The *Pocket* GARDEN TROUBLES EXPERT

Dr. D. G. Hessayon

First edition: 150,000 copies
Published 2001
by Expert Books
a division of Transworld Publishers Ltd

Copyright © Dr.D.G.Hessayon 2001

The right of Dr.D.G.Hessayon to be identified
as author of this work has been asserted in accordance
with sections 77 and 78 of the Copyright Designs and
Patents Act 1988.

A catalogue record for this book is available from the British Library

TRANSWORLD PUBLISHERS
61-63 Uxbridge Road, London W5 5SA
a division of the Random House Group Ltd

 Distributed in the United States
by Sterling Publishing Co. Inc.,
387 Park Avenue South,
New York,
NY 10016-8810

EXPERT BOOKS

CONTENTS

page

Reproduction by Spot On Digital Imaging Ltd, Perivale, Middx. UB6 7JB
Printed and bound by GGP Media GmbH

ISBN 0 903505 54 1   © D.G. HESSAYON 2001

CHAPTER 1

INTRODUCTION

What went wrong? In big gardens and small, in the hands of an expert or novice, something is bound to go wrong. Despite claims which are sometimes made, it is not possible to keep pests, disorders, diseases and weeds away from your garden by good cultivation alone. Of course, expert gardeners suffer far less than the novice because their well-grown plants are more resistant, they know how to take preventive measures and they also know how to take speedy action once trouble occurs.

This book reveals the vast array of troubles which can affect your garden. Many but not all are pests or diseases — disorders such as bolted onions and frost-damaged fruit blossom do not appear in the pest charts but are nevertheless important plant problems. In addition there are the weeds around the plants, disfiguring the beds and capable of ruining the lawn.

It is not the intention of this book to frighten you — no matter how long you garden you will never see all the troubles on the following pages. On the contrary it is the purpose of this guide to take away the worry of the unidentified problem and to tell you whether preventive measures and/or treatment are necessary.

Unfortunately you cannot ensure plant health by simply buying a sprayer and a range of bottles — pesticides are only part of the answer. Avoiding trouble in the garden begins before you buy or sow the plant and ends with the correct disposal of the dead material when its life-span is over.

It all begins when you look at the planting site. Is it in a frost pocket or dense shade? If it is then you will have to pick plants which can withstand such conditions. And spend time looking for good stock — many gardeners bring in trouble at planting time. You can sometimes avoid future trouble at the buying stage by choosing the right variety — **resistant** on the label means that it can catch the named disease but the effect will be slight, **immune** means that it cannot catch the named disease and **certified** virus-free means that the crop is susceptible to but free from the named virus. Finally there are the steps which are dealt with at length in this book — prevent troubles before they start and deal with them promptly and properly if they do arrive.

PESTS

A pest is an animal which attacks plants. Nearly all are insects (small creatures with six legs at the adult stage) and here are found the flies, caterpillars and beetles. A few small pests such as mites are often referred to as 'insects'. Some pests (e.g eelworms) are smaller than insects — others (e.g birds) are much larger.

DISEASES

A disease is a plant trouble caused by a living organism which is transmitted from one plant to another. Most diseases are caused by fungi, and these can often be prevented by spraying with a suitable chemical. The other diseases, caused by bacteria and viruses, can rarely be controlled in this way.

DISORDERS

A disorder is a plant trouble which may have disease-like symptoms, but is not caused by a living organism. Unlike diseases they are caused, not caught. Disorders indicate that something is or has been wrong with the environment — common examples are water-logging, water shortage, late frosts and shortage of a vital nutrient.

WEEDS

A weed is a plant growing in a place where you don't want it to be. The natural flora of the bed, border or lawn (the true wild flowers of your garden) are 'weeds' only because they are not wanted. Garden plants when they are in the wrong place, such as self-sown annuals in the rose bed, are also weeds.

CHAPTER 2

FLOWER TROUBLES

BORDER PERENNIALS

Rust pustules on the underside of a hollyhock leaf

For most gardeners the herbaceous or mixed border contains the largest expanse of flowers in the garden, so proper care here is most important. Thorough soil preparation is vital and enrichment with organic matter is usually necessary. When buying new plants check that they are suitable for the situation. Don't set them too close together as overcrowding encourages powdery mildew and some other diseases. Mulch and feed in the spring, and watch out for the major troubles — aphid, capsid bug, caterpillar, cutworm, slugs, grey mould, powdery mildew, virus and winter waterlogging.

BULBS

Blind narcissi — lift the bulbs and divide in autumn

Plant at the recommended time and at the right depth — setting bulbs too close to the surface can produce all leaf and few flowers. Never plant unsound bulbs, nor undersized ones if you want a good display next season. Let the leaves of spring bulbs wither before removing them. Lift hyacinths and tulips at this stage but leave daffodils in the ground unless they have started to produce lots of narrow leaves and few flowers. Watch out for the major troubles — bulb rot, narcissus fly, stem & bulb eelworm, thrips, tulip fire and virus.

BEDDING PLANTS

Cutworms sever the stems of young annuals

Good quality transplants are essential. Follow the rules when raising your own seedlings in order to avoid damping off — see The Bedding Plant Expert for details. Harden off before planting out and wait until late May with half-hardy varieties. Choose a bright site. The usual result in shady conditions is small flowers on elongated stems, but Impatiens and Begonia semperflorens will thrive. Regular dead-heading prolongs the display — use a potash-rich fertilizer if you plan to feed. Watch for the major troubles — aphid, cutworm, slugs, foot rot, cats, late frosts, inadequate watering and over-mature transplants.

ROCKERY PLANTS

Slugs are a serious menace in spring

An attractive rockery is not easy to achieve. Choose the site with care — alpines will not succeed under trees nor in poorly-drained soil. Create a level soil surface between the rocks. Use a mixture of soil, peat or peat substitute and grit at planting time. Sprinkle chippings round the plants — remove weeds before they become a nuisance. Cut back plants which start to spread and become invasive. Do not overfeed and clear away rubbish promptly. Watch out for the major troubles — ants, caterpillar, cutworm, slugs, vine weevil, grey mould, birds, winter waterlogging and drought.

Root & Bulb Troubles

Roots and fleshy underground parts are susceptible to many pests and diseases. Chafer grub, cutworm, vine weevil etc eat away at the roots, and the plants may be beyond recovery by the time the damage is obvious. Bulbs and corms may be attacked by swift moth, stem & bulb eelworm, narcissus fly and animals searching for food. The range of soil pesticides has decreased during the past few years and for most of these troubles there is no chemical answer. Some biological pest killers are available, but in the main you will have to rely on thorough cultivation and regular hoeing. In addition to these pests there are soil-borne diseases — foot rot, bulb rot, tuber rot and so on. Buy sound stock and store bulbs properly after lifting. Avoid waterlogged sites.

Bud & Flower Troubles

The pests and diseases which directly attack buds and flowers have a variety of effects — buds may fail to open (capsid bug, aphid), petals may be streaked (thrips) or eaten (earwig, caterpillar, slugs), or the blooms may be distorted (capsid bug, aphid, virus) or destroyed (grey mould, petal blight, birds, virus). In addition to these pests and diseases which directly attack the blooms there are the organisms which attack the leaves, stems and roots with the result that the quantity and quality of the floral display are reduced. Look up 'Few Flowers' (page 12) and 'No Flowers' (page 15) — you will find that the main causes of bud and flower troubles are environmental factors such as shade, water shortage, frost, poor planting etc.

Rotten bulbs and curled leaves indicate stem & bulb eelworm

Thrips cause silvery flecking of flowers in a hot summer

Leaf & Stem Troubles

Insects are the usual cause of holes and tears in the leaves. Slugs and woodlice feed at night on the lower leaves — capsid bug and a number of caterpillars attack the foliage at all levels. Most of the garden caterpillars are the larval stage of moths rather than butterflies. Aphid and powdery mildew are serious problems in a dry summer, and grey mould can be destructive when the weather is wet. Virus diseases can attack many plants — some other diseases are rather more specific. Phlox and chrysanthemum are particularly susceptible to eelworms and both antirrhinum and hollyhock are often disfigured by rust. Not all leaf and stem problems are due to insect pests and diseases — frost can cause tears in tender leaves and the death of non-hardy varieties, weedkiller drift results in distortion, nutrient deficiency can lead to leaf discoloration, and rabbits, cats and birds can wreak havoc at various stages of growth.

Yellow stripe virus on narcissus

Powdery mildew on michaelmas daisy

Rabbits are a serious herbaceous border pest in rural areas

APHID

There are many species of aphid (greenfly and blackfly) in colours ranging from white to black. Common ones include the black bean aphid and peach-potato aphid. Nearly all flowering plants may be attacked — infestations are worst in warm, settled weather. Young growth is distorted and weakened, the leaves may be twisted and discoloured and both the quality and quantity of the floral display is reduced. Infested buds may fail to open. Some aphids pose an additional threat as carriers of virus diseases. Another damaging effect is caused by the honeydew which these pests deposit on the leaves — this sticky layer becomes covered with light-robbing **sooty mould**. Spray with a greenfly killer when colonies are first seen — repeat as recommended. Organic sprays include derris, pyrethrum and horticultural soap.

BULB ROT

Basal rot

Never plant soft or mouldy bulbs and remove rotten bulbs from store. **Smoulder** causes narcissus bulbs to decay — fungal growths appear on the surface. **Basal rot** begins at the base of narcissus and lily bulbs — the brown rot spreads upwards. **Tulip fire** can be serious (see page 19) — fungal growths appear on the skin.

CAPSID BUG

These sap-sucking bugs attack dahlia, chrysanthemum and many other flowers. At first the leaves are spotted — as the foliage expands brown-edged ragged holes appear. Buds may be killed — if they open the flowers are lop-sided. Spray plants and the ground below with a contact insecticide such as pirimiphos-methyl.

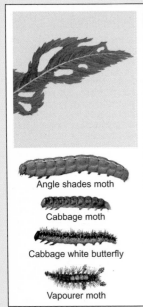

CATERPILLAR

A wide variety of leaf-eating caterpillars attack annuals and perennials in the flower garden. The 5 cm velvety smooth **angle shades moth** can be a serious nuisance on dahlia, gladiolus and many border perennials. The 3 cm smooth **cabbage moth** and the 4 cm slightly hairy **cabbage white butterfly** attack several annuals and perennials and may skeletonize the leaves. The 2.5 cm colourful and hairy **vapourer moth** is a tree and shrub pest but may damage the leaves of some border perennials. There are others, including the pink **rosy rustic moth** and the **garden tiger moth**. Pick off the caterpillars if practical — if the damage is widespread spray with an insecticide such as bifenthrin, permethrin, pirimiphos-methyl or derris. For biological control use the bacterium B. thuringiensis.

Angle shades moth

Cabbage moth

Cabbage white butterfly

Vapourer moth

CHAFER GRUB

The curved 2-4 cm grubs of the chafer beetle feed on the roots of many flowering plants between early autumn and spring. Badly affected annuals may be killed, but a serious attack is unlikely on land which is regularly cultivated. Remove grubs brought to the surface by digging, forking or hoeing.

CLUBROOT

A pest of the cabbage family which affects wallflower and stocks in the flower garden. Below the ground the roots are swollen and distorted — above the ground the plants are small and die off earlier than expected. The best precaution is to lime the soil before planting and to avoid growing wallflower on the same site year after year.

Dry rot

CORM ROT

Never plant soft or mouldy crocus or gladiolus corms — always remove rotten corms from store. Most corm rots such as **dry rot**, **hard rot** and **scab** cause brown or black spots or patches to appear on the surface. **Core rot** is quite different — it starts at the central core of gladiolus corms and then spreads outwards as a moist rot.

CUTWORM

The 5 cm green, grey or brown caterpillars live just below the soil surface. They can be a serious pest, feeding on the surface at night and severing the stems of young plants at ground level. July-August is the danger period. Hoe around healthy plants in an affected area — pick up and destroy caterpillars brought to the surface.

DAMPING OFF

The most serious seedling complaint. The base of an affected plant becomes withered and blackened — the stem topples over. There are several rules. Use sterilised compost, sow thinly and do not overwater. Start again if possible — otherwise remove affected seedlings and water the rest with Cheshunt Compound.

DOWNY MILDEW

Upper leaf surface turns yellow — greyish mould occurs below. It is less likely to be troublesome than powdery mildew in the ornamental garden, although antirrhinum, pansy, sweet pea and wallflower are often affected in wet weather. Pick off diseased leaves and reduce overcrowding. Mancozeb is the recommended fungicide.

EARWIG

A dahlia and chrysanthemum pest which feeds on flower petals at night, leaving them ragged and unsightly. Irregular holes appear on the foliage. Chemical control is not usually necessary — just shake the plants and destroy the earwigs which fall. The traditional control method is to trap them in upturned flower pots filled with straw.

FEW FLOWERS

Pests and diseases can reduce the number of blooms but the usual cause is shade — some bedding and rockery plants will hardly bloom at all in a shady environment. There are other possible causes. Planting border perennials in humus-starved soil or giving annuals too much nitrogen often leads to a poor floral display — remember that a potash-rich fertilizer is the one for flowers. Failure to harden off bedding plants or forgetting to pinch out their stem tips after planting out can result in an under-par display, and so can failure to water in dry weather. Dead-heading faded blooms is sometimes necessary to prolong the display.

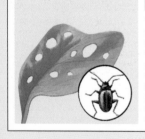

FLEA BEETLE

Tiny beetles which jump when disturbed. Small round holes appear in the young leaves of stocks, wallflower, alyssum and other members of the cabbage family. Growth is slowed down and seedlings may be killed. Water plants in dry weather — spray with derris or bifenthrin if the attack is serious.

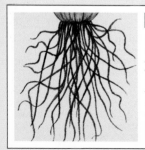

FOOT & ROOT ROT

Numerous fungi can attack the roots and stem bases. Above ground the leaves turn yellow and wilt — below ground the roots are blackened and rotten. Young and weak plants are the most susceptible. There is no cure — dig up and burn badly diseased plants, improve drainage and do not replant with the same type.

FROGHOPPER

The 6 mm immature stage of the froghopper is a sap-sucking insect. It produces a protective coating of white froth (**cuckoo spit**) on the stems of many flowering plants in May and June. Unsightly, but it causes little harm and is generally ignored. If the attack is severe wipe or hose off the cuckoo spit and spray with permethrin.

GREY MOULD

Grey mould (**botrytis**) is a fungal disease which can be destructive in wet weather. Affected areas on leaves, stems and flowers become rotten and a fluffy mould grows over the surface. Avoid poor drainage, overwatering, over-crowding and too much nitrogen. Remove badly diseased plants. Chemical control — carbendazim.

LEAF EELWORM

Various strains of microscopic worms attack a number of border perennials — chrysanthemum, aster, delphinium and peony may be killed if the infestation is severe. The leaves develop brown areas between the veins. No cure is available — lift and burn infested plants. Do not replant for 3-5 years if you are sure eelworm is present.

LEAF MINER

Winding tunnels, blisters or blotches occur on the leaves of many plants, including chrysanthe-mum and carnation — the tunnels are white at first and then turn brown. They are caused by the small grubs of various insects which feed on the leaf tissues. Spraying is not practical — pick off and burn the mined leaves.

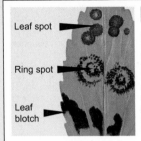

LEAF SPOT

A wide range of diseases cause leaf spotting. **Leaf spot** (round or oval spots) is seen on pansy, phlox, iris, poppy and primula. **Ring spot** (dark rings of fungal spores) is common on lupin and carnation. **Leaf blotch** (irregular-shaped patches) affects delphinium. Fungicides are ineffective — pick off diseased leaves.

Leaf spot

Ring spot

Leaf blotch

LEAFHOPPER

In summer pale flecks or patches appear on the leaves of perennials such as chrysanthemum, pelargonium and primula. Small greenish insects which jump when disturbed or their white cast-off skins can be found on the underside. Direct damage is slight and not worth bothering about, but they can transmit viruses.

LEAFY GALL

Easy to recognise — masses of short shoots and thickened leaves develop at the base of chrysanthemum, dahlia, pelargonium or phlox. It occurs in cuttings from diseased plants and is spread through wounds caused by tools. Avoid injuring stems when hoeing, destroy infected plants and do not replant with susceptible types.

LEATHERJACKET

These brownish-grey grubs can cause serious damage in a poorly-drained flower bed or border by eating the roots of seedlings or young plants. There are biological control methods, but the usual routine is to tackle the problem when digging and hoeing. Pick up and destroy the slow-moving grubs. Chemical control is not practical.

TROUBLES A-Z

FLOWERS

LILY BEETLE

The bright red beetles and their 1 cm slime-covered orange grubs should be picked off the leaves when seen — the foliage and flowers of lily, fritillaria and convallaria can be seriously damaged by this pest. Once confined to a few southern counties but it is now more widely spread. Spray with bifenthrin.

MILLEPEDE

The prime targets are the underground parts of annuals and bulbs which are diseased or damaged. The various types of millepede, both black and spotted, tend to curl up when disturbed. There are no chemicals you can use to control them — remove garden rubbish and destroy any you find when cultivating the soil.

NARCISSUS FLY

The flies lay eggs in the bulb necks of narcissus, hyacinth, iris and snowdrop as the foliage dies down. After hatching the grubs burrow into the bulbs and feed on the central core. Affected bulbs are hollow and produce few leaves and no flowers. Do not plant soft bulbs — rake soil up around the necks as leaves wither after flowering.

NO FLOWERS

The most likely cause of failure to flower is the effect of one of the factors listed in the Few Flowers section on page 12. There are one or two other possible causes. Bud drop is a common problem with sweet peas — it can be caused by bird attack but the usual reason is either a sudden change in temperature or the amount of water round the roots. **Grassiness** results in narcissus bulbs producing lots of grass-like foliage but no flowers. The commonest reason for bulbous plants failing to flower is the use of undersized offsets at planting time. With overwintering bulbs lift clumps, divide and replant if this trouble occurs.

PETAL BLIGHT

Chrysanthemum blooms can be ruined by this disease in a cold and damp summer. Small water-filled spots appear on the petals, eventually spreading and turning brown. Other plants which may be infected include anemone, dahlia and cornflower. Pick off diseased flowers — spraying with mancozeb may help.

POWDERY MILDEW

A white mealy coating covers the leaf surface. It is encouraged by overcrowding and lack of moisture at the roots. Plants which may be badly affected include michaelmas daisy, delphinium and chrysanthemum. Spray with carbendazim at the first sign of disease and 7 days later. Repeat if disease reappears.

RED SPIDER MITE

This pest is much more common under glass than outdoors, but the tiny mites on the underside of the leaves are occasionally damaging in the garden in hot and dry weather. In summer the mites are pale green, not red. Infested leaves have a dull bronze colour and fine silky webbing may be present. Spray with bifenthrin or fatty acids.

RHIZOME ROT

A serious disease of iris growing in poorly drained soil. The first sign is yellowing and withering of the leaf tips — later the fan of leaves collapses. Rhizomes develop a slimy rot. Plants can be saved if the diseased areas are cut away as soon as they are seen and the rhizomes and soil dusted with sulphur.

RUST

Raised orange, brown or black pustules appear on the leaves. Numerous plants may be attacked — common on antirrhinum, hollyhock, pelargonium, carnation, chrysanthemum and sweet william. Pick off diseased leaves, reduce overcrowding and use a high potash fertilizer. Spray with a systemic fungicide.

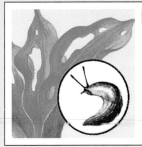

SLUGS & SNAILS

A menace in the garden, especially if the weather is wet and cool. Irregular holes appear in the leaves and tell-tale slime trails can be seen. Plants attractive to slugs include hosta, delphinium, tulip, iris, annuals and alpines. The pests hide under debris and come out at night, so clear away garden rubbish. For control see page 58.

Phlox

Narcissus

STEM & BULB EELWORM

A number of types of these tiny worms occur and each one attacks a specific group of plants. The phlox eelworm is a pest of phlox, gypsophila, evening primrose, aubretia and solidago. The young leaves of infested plants are strap-like and die off prematurely. Older leaves are distorted and few flowers appear. Several types of stem & bulb eelworm attack bulbous plants. Affected daffodil, tulip and hyacinth bulbs are soft and rotten — when cut open tell-tale dark rings can be seen inside. Foliage and flowers are pale, twisted and distorted — characteristic small yellow swellings appear on the surface of infested narcissus leaves. There are no control chemicals you can use. Dig up and burn infested plants and throw away soft and rotten bulbs. Do not replant with susceptible plants or bulbs for at least 3 years.

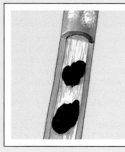

STEM ROT

A group of diseases which cause stem bases but not the roots to rot. **Sclerotinia disease** is the easiest to recognise. Wet brown rot can be seen at the base of the stem together with white fluffy mould and hard black bodies. Sunflower, dahlia, chrysanthemum and campanula can be infected. Lift diseased plants and burn.

SWIFT MOTH

A soil-living caterpillar which is easy to identify — it wriggles backwards when disturbed. It eats the roots of annuals and perennials, and burrows into all types of bulbs, corms and tubers. There is no chemical method of control, but hoeing regularly and removing nearby weeds should keep this pest under control.

THRIPS

Silvery flecking and streaking occur on flowers and leaves. The minute black or yellow flies are just visible and attacks are worst in hot weather. Gladiolus is particularly susceptible. An insecticide such as permethrin, heptenophos, horticultural soap etc can be used, but thrips are usually ignored. Water the plants during dry spells.

TUBER ROT

Dahlia tubers can be destroyed in store by fungal diseases. To prevent this from happening, stand the tubers upside down after lifting and allow them to dry. Remove any remaining soil. Place them on peat in boxes and cover roots with more peat. Store in a dry frost-free place. Inspect from time to time — cut away diseased parts.

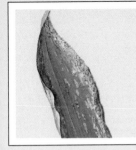

TULIP FIRE

A serious disease of tulips. Scorched areas occur on the leaves — the flowers are spotted. Young shoots are covered with a grey mould and the bulbs rot (see page 9). Cut off diseased emerging shoots below ground level — a spray with mancozeb every 2 weeks should help to prevent infection of the remaining plants.

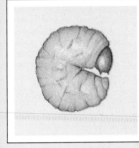

VINE WEEVIL

These wrinkled white grubs are extremely destructive underground both outdoors and under glass. The roots of many plants may be attacked, but the favourite targets are alpines and plants growing in containers. If a plant suddenly dies, look in the soil for this rolled-up grub. Imidacloprid is a long-lasting preventative.

VIRUS

Numerous viruses attack flowering plants and all sorts of distortions, discolorations and growth problems may be produced. Affected leaves may be all-yellow or they may be covered with yellow spots or patches (**mosaic**). Stems or leaves may be covered with brown stripes (**streak**) and flowers may show patches or streaks of abnormal colour (**colour break**). Leaves may be crinkled, distorted or white-veined and the plants may be killed, stunted or not noticeably affected. Viruses are carried by insects, tools or fingers and there is no cure. Buy healthy stock — destroy infected plants, but only if you are sure of the diagnosis. Do not handle healthy plants after you have touched diseased ones and do not take cuttings from virus-infected stock. Keep aphids and other sap-sucking pests under control.

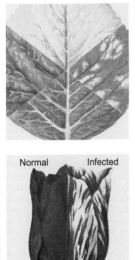

Normal   Infected

WATER LILY BEETLE

Both the beetles and their larvae are important pests of water lilies, eating out long holes in the leaves during the summer months. It can be controlled by spraying with an insecticide, but this should not be done where fish are present. It is better to hose the leaves and so wash the beetles into the water where most will drown.

WILT

The symptoms of **fusarium** and **verticillium wilt** are leaves which droop and the presence of brown staining within the stems. Suspect one of these soil-borne fungi if wilting occurs with antirrhinum, aster, sweet pea, carnation, chrysanthemum, lupin or poppy. Remove diseased plants — do not replant with susceptible flowers.

WIREWORM

These hard and shiny underground pests are a problem in new gardens and in plots adjoining grassland. They are slow moving — not active like the friendly centipede. Wireworms eat the roots of most plants and may burrow up the stems of chrysanthemum. Good soil preparation and regular cultivation are the only answer.

WOODLICE

An abundant pest in shady gardens which are not properly cared for. They hide under stones and leaves by day and devour young leaves during the night. Woodlice favour plants which have already been damaged by an earlier pest attack. Remove rubbish and sprinkle bendiocarb dust around the plants.

CHAPTER 3

TREE, SHRUB & ROSE TROUBLES

TREES & SHRUBS

Trees and shrubs are most at risk between planting and when they are fully established. Deciduous types planted in the proper way and at the proper time should have no trouble in quickly settling down. Evergreens can be more of a problem — leaf browning of newly-planted conifers can follow cold winds and bright sunshine after a frosty night. The established plant is usually capable of living a long and healthy existence provided it is hardy enough for the weather conditions and tolerant of the soil conditions. When things do go wrong it is more likely to be due to a fault in the environment rather than the effect of a specific pest or disease.

ROSES

Unlike other shrubs these plants suffer badly and regularly from disease. There are two common ones — rose mildew and rose black spot. Rose rust is much less widespread, but it can be fatal. Apart from these fungal problems there are likely to be attacks by aphids on the young shoots and flower buds. There are many other pests and diseases which afflict roses, but these are unlikely to pose a serious problem. The troubles you see are much more likely to be due to an environmental or cultural problem — poor weather, lack of nutrients, weedkiller drift, poor planting, incorrect pruning etc.

Kilmarnock willow killed by drought — water before trouble is seen

Rose leaves damaged by black spot — spray before trouble is seen

WHY PLANTS DIE

Trees and shrubs should grow and flourish for many years. Failure to survive will almost certainly be due to one of the following reasons:

Poor planting material is a common cause — avoid dried-out bare-rooted plants, and container-grown plants with densely-matted roots around the soil ball

Poor planting technique — too small a planting hole or poor consolidation of soil around container-grown plants, loose planting of bare-rooted plants, or break-up of the soil ball of container-grown or balled plants

Poor constitution of some plants can lead to failure — broom may die after a few years for no apparent reason

Wind rock — especially on exposed sites. Staking of tall specimens in such locations is essential

Waterlogged soil — poor drainage in winter can be fatal

Winter damage and spring scorch — see page 39 and page 37

Failure to water — newly-planted specimens should be watered in and woody plants during the first season in the garden should be thoroughly watered during prolonged dry weather in summer

One of the fatal pests or diseases — included here are dieback, silver leaf, fireblight, honey fungus, phytophthora rot, clematis wilt, dutch elm disease, rose rust and canker

Weedkiller damage — a rare cause of death, but a few general herbicides such as sodium chlorate can be fatal if allowed to creep into the soil around the roots

Fireblight — a devastating disease of the rose family

Canker — a common cause of death of ornamental and fruit trees

WHY PLANTS FAIL TO FLOWER

There are many possible reasons why a flowering shrub or tree fails to bloom — the following list covers the main causes:

Too much shade Many flowering shrubs are sun-lovers and will produce leaves but no flowers if the light intensity is too low. Check the plant in The Tree & Shrub Expert — if full sun is required you will have to cut back surrounding foliage or move the plant

Impatience It is quite normal for some trees and shrubs to take several years after planting before coming into flower — wisteria, yucca and camellia are examples. A few such as tulip tree may take many years before flowering starts

Dryness at the roots Drought will delay the onset of flowering and can also cause bud and blossom drop. Drought is a common cause of poor berry production. A long period of soil dryness in summer can result in poor flowering in the following year

Poor pruning Drastic pruning at the wrong time of year is an all-too-common cause of the production of non-flowering shoots

Frost damage to flower buds The buds and blossoms of a large range of woody plants can be killed by late spring frosts

Disease In some seasons blossom wilt (page 26) causes the unopened flowers of ornamental cherry to wither and die

Balling A problem affecting some rose varieties in wet weather — see page 26

Birds Bullfinches occasionally strip the buds from forsythia and ornamental cherry

WHY PLANTS BECOME LANKY

Lanky growth is a common sight in the shrub border and rose garden. The stems are taller and laxer than normal and the foliage is sparser than it should be. There are three basic causes:

Too much shade Under shady conditions the stem growth of many shrubs becomes spindly with longer spaces than normal between the leaves. Always check the light requirements of a plant before buying

Neglect Some trees and shrubs require little or no pruning and so they suffer few ill-effects if neglected. Many others, however, require cutting back every year to remove older wood. Always check the pruning requirements of a plant before buying

Old age Some shrubs such as lilac tend to become lanky after many years with long lengths of bare stem beneath a crown of leaves. Cut back all the branches to dormant side shoots. One year's flowering has to be sacrificed but bushy growth will be restored

Leaf & Stem Troubles

Poor care and poor growing conditions can seriously affect the leaves and shoots of woody plants. A number of disorders are described in the A-Z section — summer drought, winter damage, spring scorch, etc and you will find others in Chapter 9. In addition to these disorders there are the pests and diseases which attack trees, shrubs and roses. Aphids can be a problem on honeysuckle, ornamental cherry and roses, and leaf-eating caterpillars such as the magpie moth are occasionally troublesome. These are exceptions — most of the insect pests are not often serious and control measures are only necessary if they are unusually numerous or you are an extremely keen gardener. Similarly, the diseases of leaves and stems are often disfiguring rather than destructive, but there are important exceptions. Fireblight, clematis wilt, rose rust, dieback and silver leaf can all be fatal, and rose black spot, rose mildew and peach leaf curl are extremely damaging.

Trunk & Bark Troubles

There is no clear-cut distinction between stem and trunk troubles, but the pests and diseases of the trunks and bark of trees should be taken seriously as some can be fatal. You can often cut back a diseased or damaged shoot to healthy wood, but there may be no way of dealing with a diseased or badly damaged tree trunk. Dutch elm disease decimated our elm tree population and phytophthora rot is now destroying countless ornamental cherry trees and their relatives. Coral spot can be a killer, and so can canker, honey fungus and fireblight.

Silver leaf on ornamental plum

Coral spot on judas tree

24

ADELGID

Conifers are attacked by these black aphid-like insects and young trees can be badly affected. In summer dense tufts of white woolly growths are produced on the underside of the leaves and conspicuous galls may be produced. Bifenthrin can be sprayed in late winter, but treatment is rarely necessary on mature trees.

APHID

The commonest and most serious of all rose pests. The first clusters of greenfly feed on the sap of tender young shoots in spring and vigour is seriously reduced. Shoots and leaves are distorted and infested buds may fail to open. Sticky honeydew is secreted and this is soon covered by a black fungus (**sooty mould**). Aphids may be orange, red, green or black and few shrubs or trees are immune. Each species has its own range of host plants — this may be restricted to just one or two (e.g juniper aphid) or there may be a wide variety of susceptible garden plants (e.g peach-potato aphid). Spraying before aphids become serious is recommended for roses — use a systemic insecticide such as heptenophos or a contact one such as bifenthrin, pirimicarb, derris or horticultural soap. Repeat as instructed if aphids return.

BACTERIAL CANKER

This canker affects ornamental plum, almond and cherry. Gum oozes from the infected area and the foliage develops brown circular spots which fall out to leave a shot-hole effect. Attacked branches soon die — cut out diseased wood and spray the trees with a copper compound in August, September and October.

BALLING

Rose buds develop normally, but the petals fail to open properly and then turn brown. It is usually due to the effect of wet weather on varieties with large, thin-petalled blooms. Balling is always worst in a shady area where the buds are shielded from the drying rays of the sun. It can also be caused by a heavy aphid attack.

BLINDNESS

An empty wheat-like husk appears instead of a flower bud on top of a rose stem. There are several possible causes — late frosts, root damage, lack of nutrients or water and too much shade have all been blamed. Cut the stem back to a strong bud which should then produce a shoot which will flower in the normal way.

BLOSSOM WILT

In a mild and wet spring this disease can be serious on crab apple and ornamental cherry trees. Blossom and leaf trusses wilt and turn brown — a grey-coloured mould may spread over the surface. Remove infected blossoms and spurs in spring. Carbendazim applied in late spring will help to prevent trouble next year.

BUD BLAST

Infected rhododendron flower buds turn brown and are covered with black fungal bristles. They do not rot and remain firmly attached — frost-damaged buds are soft and easily pulled away. Remove diseased buds and burn. Leafhopper damage is responsible — prevent attacks by spraying with a greenfly killer in August.

CANKER

A general term for a diseased area on the bark. The canker is usually cracked and sunken, and will kill the branch if neglected and allowed to encircle it. Some attack a wide range of woody plants — others are specific. Rose canker can be a problem. Take care when hoeing — cut out and burn all of the diseased wood.

CAPSID BUG

Small insects which move rapidly when disturbed. They feed on many shrubs with rose as the favourite host. Small brown spots appear on young leaves, turning into ragged holes as the foliage expands. Damaged buds turn brown and wither. Rarely serious enough to need treatment — use a systemic insecticide if necessary.

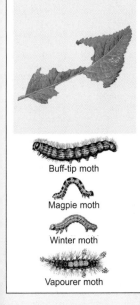

Buff-tip moth

Magpie moth

Winter moth

Vapourer moth

CATERPILLAR

Leaf-eating caterpillars are more serious on trees, shrubs and roses than in the flower garden — some species of these pests form large colonies and all the leaves on a shrub may be stripped with only the veins remaining. The 5 cm **buff-tip moth** attacks numerous trees, some shrubs and roses. The black and yellow 'looper' caterpillar of the **magpie moth** is smaller but is also more damaging — some shrubs may be defoliated. The green 'looper' **winter moth** devours young leaves and may spin them together and the 2.5 cm colourful **vapourer moth** feeds on trees, shrubs and roses from May to August. Pick off caterpillars if practical — if the damage is widespread spray with an insecticide such as bifenthrin, permethrin, pirimiphos-methyl or derris. For tent-making caterpillars see page 38.

CHAFER BEETLE

The grub eats roots and the adult beetle bites irregular-shaped holes in leaves. They range in size from the 1 cm garden chafer to the 4 cm cockchafer — the smaller chafer beetles sometimes attack rose buds resulting in one-sided blooms. Treatment is not usually required — spray with bifenthrin if necessary.

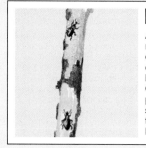

CLAY-COLOURED WEEVIL

A small brown weevil which bites notches out of the leathery leaves of rhododendron, camellia, laurel etc. The bark may also be gnawed, leading to the death of the shoot. Conifers are another host for this pest. Control is not easy. Hoe the surrounding soil and spray both the tree and ground with permethrin. Biological controls are available.

CLEMATIS WILT

A destructive fungal disease of clematis, especially young plants of large-flowered varieties. Shoots wilt and then suddenly collapse and die. Cut out affected shoots — new ones often develop from the base. Spray new growth with carbendazim. When hoeing around clematis make sure that the stems are not damaged.

CORAL SPOT

Raised pink spots appear on the branches. Dead wood is the breeding ground for the fungus, and the air-borne spores infect living trees and shrubs through wounds. The effect can be fatal, so never leave dead wood laying about. Cut out affected areas, going well beyond the patch of pink pustules on the bark. Burn all prunings.

TREES, SHRUBS & ROSES

CROWN GALL

Brown and warty outgrowths sometimes occur on the lower stems and roots of trees and shrubs. This bacterial disease is worst on young specimens in badly-drained soil. Mature trees are not usually harmed but a ring of galls around the stem base can be serious. Cut out infected area and spray with a copper fungicide.

DIEBACK

Shoots may die back, beginning at the tip and progressing steadily downwards, for a number of reasons. The cause may be a disease, such as canker, rose mildew or rose black spot, or there may be a cultural problem such as drought, waterlogging or nutrient deficiency. Cut off and burn the affected shoot.

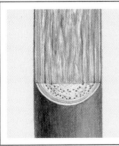

DUTCH ELM DISEASE

The first sign of trouble is yellowing of the foliage during the summer months. The leaves turn brown but remain hanging on the tree. The shoots of the dead branches are hooked at the tip. Cut off all diseased branches. If the tree is badly infected or dead, dig out and burn. Never leave diseased wood laying about in the garden.

FALSE SILVER LEAF

A common disease which at first glance looks like silver leaf (see page 37). Leaves are silvery, but the effect appears all over the tree and not progressively along a branch. A cut branch reveals that the staining of silver leaf disease is absent. The cause of false silver leaf is irregular watering or nutrient deficiency. Mulch in spring.

FASCIATION

Shoots of roses and some shrubs are occasionally abnormally wide and flattened, giving the appearance of a number of shoots fused together. Despite this deformity leaf and flower development are unaffected. It is caused by damage to the growing point — cut off the abnormal branch and the shrub will grow quite normally.

FIREBLIGHT

A devastating disease of shrubs and trees of the rose family. The tell-tale sign is the presence of brown wilted leaves which do not fall. Cankers develop on the bark and diseased shoots die back — cut out affected branches to 60 cm below the brown leaves. Trees die when the trunk is infected — remove and burn.

FROGHOPPER

White frothy masses appear on the shoots of roses and some shrubs in May and June. Inside this froth lives the small sap-sucking froghopper. This **cuckoo spit** may be unsightly, but it causes little harm to mature plants and is generally ignored. If the attack is severe wipe or hose off and spray with permethrin or derris.

Oak apple

GALLS

These swellings on shrubs and trees are caused by the plant's reaction to the irritation caused by insects or fungi. Some are large and colourful — in nearly all cases there is little or no harm to the plant. Crown gall (page 29) is the commonest — others include **oak apple**, **azalea gall**, **purse gall** and **pouch gall**.

TREES, SHRUBS & ROSES

HONEY FUNGUS

A common cause of the death of shrubs and trees. A white fan of fungal growth occurs below the bark near ground level. On roots black 'bootlaces' are found. Toadstools appear in autumn at the base. Burn diseased stems and roots and replant with non-woody types. A phenolic soil drench may reduce spread.

LEAF BEETLE

These 5 mm long beetles feed on the soft tissue of willow and poplar leaves during the summer months. As a result the foliage is skeletonized rather than holed, but the damage is rarely severe and remedial measures are not worthwhile. Use a contact insecticide such as bifenthrin or derris if spraying is necessary.

LEAF-CUTTER BEE

The tell-tale sign is a series of semi-circular holes cut out of the leaf edges of several types of trees and shrubs. Roses are the usual host, but lilac, laburnum, wisteria and privet may also be attacked. These 1 cm hairy bees do not live in colonies and the damage they do is not normally serious enough to require spraying.

LEAF MINER

Blisters or long winding mines are produced by small grubs feeding on the tissues within the leaf. Many trees and shrubs can be affected, including holly, lilac, rose, privet, honeysuckle, azalea and birch. Pick off and destroy damaged leaves, but it is a minor problem so spraying with a systemic insecticide is rarely worthwhile.

31

LEAF-ROLLING SAWFLY

Greyish-green grubs feed inside the tightly-rolled leaves on rose bushes. The affected leaves may shrivel and die — the problem can be serious on roses grown near to trees. You can prevent damage by spraying with permethrin in May, but you will have to use a systemic insecticide once a serious attack has occurred.

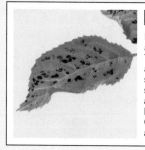

LEAF SPOT

Many shrubs and trees are attacked by this type of disease. The usual cause is fungal infection, and the disease may have a specific name — **azalea leaf spot**, **sycamore tar spot**, **willow anthracnose** etc. Gather up and burn diseased leaves in autumn. Control is difficult, but you can try a copper or mancozeb spray.

LEAF WEEVIL

Metallic green or brown 5 mm weevils may appear on birch, beech, oak, mountain ash etc in early summer. They occur in large numbers and produce irregular holes in the foliage. Control measures are rarely necessary as they move off after a few days — if spraying is needed use bifenthrin or pirimiphos-methyl.

LEAFHOPPER

Small greenish insects which jump when disturbed or their white cast-off skins can be found on the underside of the leaves. Pale mottled patches cover the upper surface. Growth is checked — leaf fall occurs after a bad attack. Not usually treated, but spray with a systemic insecticide if the problem is serious.

TREES, SHRUBS & ROSES

LOSS OF VARIEGATION

Many shrubs bear yellow and green patterned leaves ('variegata') or green, yellow and red leaves ('tricolor'). In dense shade the green areas spread and the variegation is diminished. Even in good light there is often a tendency for all-green branches to appear. These reverted areas should be cut out immediately.

PEACH LEAF CURL

This serious disease of ornamental cherries, almonds etc leads to early leaf fall and weakening of the tree. The leaves are infected in spring and large reddish blisters develop. The fungus overwinters between the bud scales and not on fallen leaves, so spray with mancozeb in mid-February, 2 weeks later and again at leaf fall.

PHYTOPHTHORA ROT

The soil fungus first kills the roots around the main stem, later spreading to other roots. The bark and the roots in the affected area are usually blackened. An important disease of ornamental cherries and many other trees — leaves are small and sparse, stems die back. Avoid waterlogged sites. There is no cure — dig out and burn.

POWDERY MILDEW

White powdery patches appear on the leaves of trees and shrubs — common on clematis, crab apple, euonymus, hawthorn, mahonia and willow. It is encouraged by overcrowding and dry soil. Repeat spraying with carbendazim will help — cut off and burn badly diseased shoots in autumn. For details of rose mildew see page 35.

RED SPIDER MITE

The presence of fine silky webbing on the leaves and an unhealthy bronze colour are the tell-tale signs of these tiny spider-like mites. They may infest the underside of rose, conifers and other shrubs and trees in hot, settled weather but are rarely numerous enough to pose a problem. Derris every 3 weeks is the spray recommendation.

RHODODENDRON BUG

Shiny brown insects with lacy wings feed on the underside of rhododendron leaves. The foliage is mottled above and turns rusty brown below — the leaf edges turn downwards. It is encouraged by dry weather and spraying is occasionally necessary. Use a permethrin spray in late spring and repeat 1 month later.

ROSE BLACK SPOT

The tell-tale signs are black spots with yellow edges. As the disease develops the yellow areas spread, premature leaf fall takes place and stems may die back. The fungus overwinters on stems and fallen leaves — infection takes place early in the season although the symptoms may not be clearly visible until July. The severity of the attack depends on the variety (shrub roses are usually less resistant than modern hybrids), the location (pure air encourages the disease) and the growing conditions (black spot thrives in warm, wet weather). It is difficult to control. Remove and burn fallen leaves and cut off black-spotted stems when pruning. Spraying is necessary with susceptible varieties. Apply myclobutanil when leaf buds are opening and repeat 7 days later. Spray again when first spots appear — repeat every 2 weeks.

TREES, SHRUBS & ROSES

ROSE MILDEW

This form of powdery mildew is the most widespread rose disease. A white, powdery mould develops on leaves, buds and shoots. Affected leaves curl and may fall prematurely — diseased buds may not open properly. The disease is encouraged by closed-in conditions, dryness at the roots, poor feeding and by hot days which are followed by cold nights. Climbers growing against walls are especially susceptible — ensure there is adequate air space between the wires and the bricks. Some roses are much more resistant than others — check before buying. Cut off and burn badly infected shoots when pruning, use a balanced and not a nitrogen-rich fertilizer when feeding and mulch in spring. Spray with myclobutanil or carbendazim when the first spots are seen — repeat every 2 weeks.

ROSE RUST

Not common, but it is often fatal when it strikes. Orange swellings which turn black in August appear on the underside of the leaves. New shoots turn reddish and shrivel. It is encouraged by a cold spring following a hard winter and by potash shortage in the soil. Apply myclobutanil when first seen — repeat as directed.

ROSE SICKNESS

If the site has grown roses for more than 10 years then it is liable to be rose-sick. The old roses on the site may show little or no ill-effects, but planting a new rose in such soil can result in poor growth (**replant disease**). For this reason the topsoil in the planting area should be changed. If it is not practical to provide new soil (50 x 50 x 50 cm for each new rose to be planted) then you can help matters by adding a liberal amount of compost or well-rotted manure plus a dressing of high-nitrogen fertilizer to the remaining soil before planting. This should reduce but not eliminate the effect of replant disease.

ROSE SLUGWORM

This yellowish-green 15 mm sawfly grub can sometimes be seen feeding on the upper surface of rose leaves. Neither the veins nor the lower surface skin are eaten — the filmy area dries out and turns brown. The grubs are readily killed by an insecticide such as bifenthrin or derris, but treatment is rarely necessary.

RUST

Yellow or brown raised spots appear on the leaves of many shrubs and trees — spore-producing pustules occur on the underside. It occurs on birch, rhododendron, mahonia, willow and conifers. Spraying with myclobutanil or mancozeb is rarely necessary, but rose rust (page 35) must be treated.

SCALE

A number of different scale varieties occur on tree branches, but their lifestyle is generally the same. The adults spend their lives in one place, protected by a hard shell. Their feeding causes leaf yellowing and loss of vigour. Common ones include **brown scale**, **mussel scale** and **yew scale** (illustrated). Spray with bifenthrin in May.

SHOT HOLE BORER

Several types of shot hole borer or **bark beetle** attack ornamental trees — the **elm bark beetle** carrying dutch elm disease (page 29) is the best known. Small round holes appear in the bark and the layer beneath is usually mined with tunnels. There is no cure. Maintain good growing conditions and remove damaged branches.

TREES, S RUBS & ROSES

SHOT HOLE DISEASE

Brown spots appear on the leaves of ornamental cherry and laurel — as the leaves expand these brown areas fall out and are replaced by round holes scattered over the surface. This fungus disease favours trees which have been weakened by poor growing conditions — the answer is to water, feed and mulch properly.

SILVER LEAF

The spores enter through wounds and the first sign is a silvery look to the leaves. It is a serious disease of ornamental cherry — other hosts include laburnum, hawthorn, willow and rhododendron (leaves not silvered). Dieback occurs and wood is stained. Cut back to clean wood before July — dig out bracket toadstools if they appear

SPLIT BARK

A common cause of cracks appearing in the bark is severe frost — it is not uncommon for the base of rhododendron to be split in this way. But splitting can occur at any time of the year — poor growing conditions can cause this problem. Cut away any wood which is rotten — feed and mulch to improve vigour.

SPRING SCORCH

The least understood of early spring problems. Cold-induced drought leads to the browning or death of evergreens — sunshine and drying winds stimulate water loss but the roots are not yet active enough to satisfy the demand. Protect from east winds if you can — spray newly-planted evergreens with water in spring.

SUMMER DROUGHT

The first stage is wilting, which is reversible if watered promptly. The next stage is browning and then leaf drop, which can be fatal with evergreens. Watering is practical with newly-planted specimens or if the roots are shallow — the long-term answer is to improve the water-holding capacity of the soil before planting. Mulch in spring.

TENT CATERPILLAR

Lackey moth (illustrated), **brown-tail moth** and **small ermine moth** produce a tent of silken webs within which the caterpillars feed on the foliage. Pick off the tents or cut off the affected shoots if practical — if the attack is severe spray the plants with a contact insecticide such as bifenthrin, pirimiphos-methyl or derris.

THRIPS

Thrips can be found on many trees and shrubs but they are only likely to be an important pest on roses. Petal edges are blackened — flowers and leaves are mottled and malformed. These minute 4-winged insects (**thunder flies**) are associated with hot, thundery weather. Keep plants watered — spray with derris.

TORTRIX MOTH

Small brown or green caterpillars (**rose maggots**) spin leaf edges or adjacent leaves together with fine silken threads. Within this protective cover the caterpillars feed on the leaf tissues. May and June are the most likely time of attack. Pick off and destroy rolled leaves. Not easy to control by spraying, but you can try bifenthrin.

VINE WEEVIL

The grubs are a serious pest of pot plants. With trees and shrubs it is the beetle which is an occasional nuisance. Small U-shaped notches are cut out of the leaf edges of leathery shrubs such as rhododendron, azalea, laurel and camellia. If necessary spray the plants and soil with a systemic insecticide.

VIRUS

Viruses are carried by insects, tools and fingers. There are many symptoms — yellow-blotched, yellow-lined or crinkled leaves, stunted growth, streaked flowers etc. There is no cure, so it is fortunate that very few trees and shrubs are susceptible to serious attack. Buy healthy stock — keep aphids under control.

WINTER DAMAGE

Many trees and shrubs are at risk in a severe winter, especially if they are slightly tender or newly planted. They can be damaged in several ways — waterlogging in an abnormally wet season can lead to root rot, heavy frost can cause brown blotches at the tips of leaves and deep snow can break the branches of evergreens.

WITCHES' BROOM

A dense cluster of branching twigs can sometimes be seen on the trunks and main branches of birch, cherry and conifers. The cause is usually a fungus, but the culprit may be a virus or a change in the structure of a growth bud. These clumps do no harm to the tree, but they can be cut off if they are unsightly.

CHAPTER 4

VEGETABLE TROUBLES

BEANS & PEAS

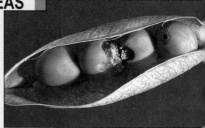

Pea moth

The main threat to the crop depends on the type you grow. Aphid is the major pest of broad beans and chocolate spot is the most serious disease. The chief problem with runner beans is the failure of pods to set — see page 54. French beans can be attacked by numerous pests and diseases but they are rarely serious. Peas do have two important problems — birds and pea moth caterpillars.

BRASSICAS

Mealy aphid

Included here are cabbage, cauliflower, brussels sprouts, kale, broccoli, turnip, swede and radish. Kale and radish are usually trouble-free but the rest are subject to a wide range of pests, diseases and disorders. The worst of these troubles are cabbage root fly, mealy aphid, whitefly, clubroot, flea beetle and pigeons. In addition there are numerous cultural problems — failure to consolidate the soil and to plant firmly can lead to heartless cabbages, blown sprouts and button-sized cauliflowers. The root brassicas are generally much healthier than the leafy ones, but powdery mildew and gall weevil can be extra problems.

CARROTS & PARSNIPS

Carrot fly

Carrots are not an easy crop to grow. If your soil is heavy choose a short-rooted variety, but this won't help against carrot fly — in some areas attacks by this pest make growing this vegetable hardly worthwhile. Other problems which are occasionally serious include splitting, aphids and sclerotinia rot in store. Parsnips are less susceptible than carrots to pests — canker is the major disease.

LETTUCES

With outdoor lettuce you must guard against soil pests, slugs and birds — in cool, damp weather the two major diseases (downy mildew and grey mould) can be destructive. Remember that any check to growth can lead to bolting — see page 45. Lettuce grown under glass is even more vulnerable to disease attack — water with care and do not soak unless the compost surface is dry.

ONIONS & LEEKS

Stem & bulb eelworm

Only four onion problems are likely to seriously trouble the gardener. They are onion fly, stem & bulb eelworm, neck rot and white rot. Raise onions from sets if you have been troubled by onion fly in the past. There are several disorders, including splitting (saddleback), bolting and bull neck. Leeks are less prone to pest and disease attack than onions.

POTATOES

Leaf curl virus

Many pests, diseases and disorders can attack potatoes and reduce yields, but only four are likely to be a serious threat. Three of them are pests — potato cyst eelworm, keeled slug and wireworm. The other serious problem is a disease — potato blight. Virus diseases can be a menace but it is easy to avoid trouble by using seed potatoes which are virus-free. The major disorder is frost damage — late spring frosts can severely damage the young shoots of early varieties.

SPINACH & BEETROOT

Bolting can be a problem with both of these vegetables and so can trace element deficiency. Beetroot is also susceptible to black bean aphid and mangold fly but yields are not usually seriously affected. It is an easy crop to grow, but downy mildew and spinach blight caused by the cucumber mosaic virus make spinach a difficult vegetable for many gardeners.

TOMATOES & CUCUMBERS

Blossom end rot

The list of troubles is a long one — pests and diseases include aphids, grey mould, damping off, mildews, eelworms, viruses, stem foot and root rots, wilts, whiteflies, red spider mites etc. Keep a careful watch and treat plants immediately symptoms are seen. The fruits can suffer from many disorders such as splitting, blossom end rot, greenback, dry set, bitterness, withering and so on — common causes are incorrect watering, trace element deficiency and dry air under glass.

ANTHRACNOSE

A disease of beans and cucumber. Green or brown sunken spots appear on the pods or fruit — the affected areas turn pink. There are brown patches on the leaves and the stems may be cankered — in a bad attack the plants are killed. Remove diseased leaves and fruit — lift and destroy badly diseased bean plants.

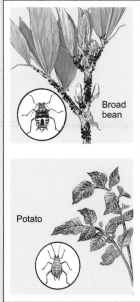

Broad bean

Potato

APHID

You may find greenfly or blackfly on many different vegetables, but the severity of the attack depends on the type of vegetable grown as well as the weather. The black bean aphid is the most serious of all broad bean pests — stunting growth, damaging the flowers and distorting pods. Onions, on the other hand, are avoided by greenfly. Infestations are worst in hot, settled weather — carrot leaves are discoloured, lettuce is puckered and blackened, and potato leaflets turn brown. In some cases aphids do far more harm by spreading virus diseases than by sucking sap from the host plants. The answer is to spray thoroughly with an insecticide such as bifenthrin as soon as the colonies begin to build up — repeat as instructed if the weather remains warm and dry. Horticultural soap, derris and rape oil are organic sprays.

BEAN SEED FLY

All bean varieties are susceptible to these 5 mm long white grubs. The damaged seeds may fail to germinate — if they do they are weakened and distorted. Damage is worst when growth is slow, so early crops and those grown in cold wet soil are the worst affected. Plant compost-raised seedlings to avoid damage.

BITTERNESS

If the fruits of an outdoor cucumber look normal but the taste is distinctly bitter then one of the growing conditions is at fault. A sudden drop or increase in temperature or soil moisture can be to blame and so can the use of too much nitrogen. Try to maintain even growth by careful watering and balanced feeding. The second type of bitterness is associated with misshapen club-like cucumbers grown under glass. Here the cause is pollination — remember that male flowers must be removed. This tedious job can be avoided by growing an all-female variety such as Pepinex.

BLACKLEG

The tell-tale sign of this bacterial disease of potatoes is the blackening of the stems at and below ground level. The leaves turn yellow and wilt — eventually the haulm withers. It is carried in the tubers so never plant seed potatoes which are soft and rotten. It is worst in heavy soil and wet weather — destroy infected plants.

BLOSSOM END ROT

A leathery dark-coloured patch occurs at the bottom of tomatoes — it is nearly always restricted to greenhouse crops and to the first few trusses at the start of the season. The cause is poor calcium uptake because of irregular watering — never let the compost dry out in growing bags. Small-fruited varieties are rarely affected.

BLOTCHY RIPENING

Parts of the fruit of greenhouse tomatoes remain yellow or orange and they fail to ripen — the usual cause is too much sunshine or too little potash in the soil. **Greenback** appears for the same reasons — the area around the stalk remains hard, green and unripe. Apply shading and feed with a high-potash fertilizer.

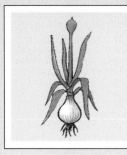

BOLTING

Several vegetables may flower and run to seed before they have reached the harvesting stage — onions, beetroot, celery, lettuce and spinach are the usual ones. Common causes are sowing or planting too early, shortage of water and abnormally cold spring weather. Look for varieties which are bolt-resistant when buying seed.

BULL NECK

The production of abnormally thick necks is a serious onion complaint as the bulbs will not store properly. Sowing seed too deeply can be responsible and so can using too much manure or applying too much nitrogen. Use a liquid feed during the growing season — choose one such as tomato fertilizer which is potash-rich.

CABBAGE CATERPILLAR

Holes appear in the leaves of brassicas such as cabbage, cauliflower and broccoli. The 2.5 cm **small cabbage white** is velvety — the 4 cm **large cabbage white** is slightly hairy and the **cabbage moth** is smooth. Attacks are worst in hot, dry weather. Pick off if practical or spray with bifenthrin or derris.

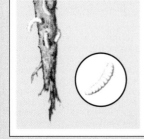

CABBAGE ROOT FLY

The tell-tale sign is blue-tinged foliage which wilts in sunny weather — recent transplants are particularly susceptible. Small maggots eat the roots, leaving a blackened stump. Young plants are killed, older cabbages fail to heart and cauliflowers form tiny heads. Apply chlorpyriphos immediately after transplanting.

CAPSID

Greenish 5 mm insects feeding on the leaves produce small brown spots which later turn into holes. Young shoots may be distorted and there may be pronounced crinkling of young leaflets, but damage is usually not serious enough to affect yield. If the attack is severe spray the plants and ground with a contact insecticide.

CARROT FLY

The tell-tale sign is reddish foliage which wilts in sunny weather — at a later stage the leaves turn yellow. The 5 mm maggots are a serious pest of carrot, parsnip and celery — seedlings are killed, mature roots are riddled. Delay sowing maincrop carrots until June — lift as soon as practical. Sow thinly — destroy all thinnings.

CELERY FLY

White 5 mm maggots tunnel within the leaves of celery, carrot and parsnip causing blisters to develop. Attacks occur from April onwards, and the effect is most serious on young plants. Leaves may shrivel and die — celery stalks are stunted and bitter. Remove affected leaves — spray with a systemic fungicide if serious.

CELERY HEART ROT

This disease is noticed after lifting — on cutting the plant open the heart is found to be a slimy brown mass. The bacteria which produce the rot enter the stalks through wounds caused by slugs, frost or careless cultivation. Grow celery on well-drained land which was not affected last year — keep slugs under control.

CELERY LEAF SPOT

Brown spots of this fungal disease appear first on the outer leaflets and then spread to all the foliage. In a wet season the whole plant may be destroyed. Prevent infection by purchasing treated seed or by never planting seedlings with spotted leaves. Spray with carbendazim at the first sign of disease — repeat as necessary.

CHOCOLATE SPOT

A destructive disease of broad bean which appears as small brown spots on the leaves and dark streaks along the stems. Pods may be affected. In a bad attack the plant is killed. Prevention involves leaving adequate space between plants. Destroy infected plants and spray the rest with carbendazim.

CLUBROOT

The tell-tale sign of this brassica disease is discoloured foliage which wilts in sunny weather. Roots become swollen — it can be disastrous in a wet season. Ensure land is free-draining and well limed before planting — dip transplants in thiophanate methyl solution. Do not use land for brassicas for several years.

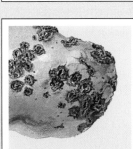

COMMON SCAB

Scurfy patches appear on potatoes — in a severe attack the whole surface may be covered. It is only skin deep, so the eating quality after peeling is unaffected. It is encouraged by dry weather and sandy soil. To avoid trouble dig in compost and do not lime before planting. Grow a resistant variety (e.g Maris Peer).

CUTWORM

The 5 cm grey, green or brown caterpillars live just below the surface. Young plants of vegetables such as lettuce, cabbage, cauliflower etc are severed at ground level. Leaves and roots may also be eaten. Hoe around the plants regularly — destroy caterpillars which are brought to the surface.

DAMPING OFF

The most serious seedling complaint. The base becomes withered and the stem topples over. Under glass use sterilised compost, sow thinly and do not overwater. Outdoors avoid sowing in cold, wet soil. Start again if possible — otherwise remove affected seedlings and water the rest with Cheshunt Compound.

DOWNY MILDEW

Pea

Lettuce

A leaf disease which affects a wide range of vegetables. Discoloured blotches appear on the upper surface and below them on the undersurface are grey or purple mouldy areas — these patches may spread to cover the whole surface. It thrives in cool and wet conditions. On peas and beans the undersurface patches are pale purple and the infected pods are spotted and distorted. On members of the cabbage family the underleaf patches are white and furry — it is usually restricted to young plants. It can be serious on lettuce — large pale patches appear between the veins on the upper leaf surface of older leaves. Onion leaves shrivel from the tips and the bulbs are soft. Practise crop rotation. Avoid overcrowding. Do not overwater seedlings. Spray with mancozeb and repeat every 2 weeks.

DRY SET

The growth of the tomato fruitlet ceases when it reaches the size of a match-head — it becomes dry and brown. Hot, dry air at pollination time is the cause — cold nights and dry air at pollination time results in **chats** (undersize tomatoes). Prevention calls for misting the foliage in the morning when the weather is hot.

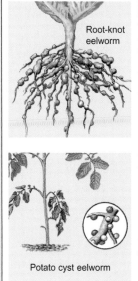

Root-knot eelworm

Potato cyst eelworm

EELWORM

These microscopic worm-like creatures (**nematodes**) live in the soil and can be a menace to a number of vegetables. There are several types with their particular list of hosts. **Root-knot eelworm** causes gall-like growths on the roots of cucumber, lettuce, tomato and french beans. Leaves are discoloured — growth is stunted. **Potato cyst eelworm** produces pinhead-sized cysts on the roots of tomato and potato. Leaves wilt, growth is stunted and potato haulm dies down prematurely. **Stem & bulb eelworm** causes distorted leaves which are often swollen — onion is the main host but peas, beans and carrots may be attacked. There is no cure for eelworm. Lift and burn infested plants — do not grow susceptible varieties in the soil which is infested with eelworm for at least 6 years.

FANGING

The roots of carrot and beetroot may be forked for a number of reasons. The usual cause is the addition of manure or compost to the soil shortly before sowing. Other causes are growing the crop in stony soil or in heavy ground which has not been properly cultivated. Use land which has been manured for a previous crop.

FLEA BEETLE

A pest of seedlings of the cabbage family which can be serious during warm and dry spells in April and May. Small round holes can be seen in the leaves and growth may be checked. The tiny beetles jump when disturbed. Spray or dust with derris when the first attacks are noticed. Water if the weather is dry.

FOOT & ROOT ROT

The leaves discolour and wilt — the roots and stem bases turn brown or black. Susceptible vegetables include tomatoes, cucumbers, peas and beans — young plants are most at risk. There is no cure. Burn badly affected plants. Water the rest with Cheshunt Compound. Rotate crops. Avoid overwatering.

FUSARIUM WILT

A fungal disease of french and runner beans. The outward signs are wilted stems, yellowing leaves and few pods. If the stem of an infected plant is cut open the tell-tale sign is revealed — reddish-brown longitudinal streaks through the stem tissue. Remove and burn affected plants. Next time grow a resistant variety.

GALL WEEVIL

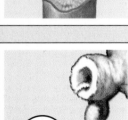

These swellings on the roots of the brassica family can be mistaken for clubroot (page 47), but when cut open they are hollow with a maggot inside. The swellings are generally close to the soil surface. Gall weevil is less common and less serious than clubroot — the effect on yield is slight. Control measures are not worthwhile.

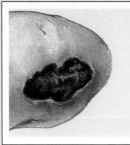

GANGRENE

A storage disease of potatoes. Dark brown depressions occur on the surface — the insides are decayed and hollow. **Dry rot** is another storage disease — shrunken areas with whitish pustules appear on the surface. There is no cure for these problems — only store potatoes which are sound and destroy diseased ones.

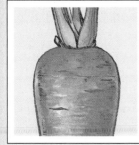

GREEN TOP

The tops of carrots are sometimes found to be green when the crop is harvested. Unlike green potato tubers these carrots are not harmful but they are unsightly. Green top is caused by sunlight on the exposed crowns — it is easily prevented by earthing-up to cover the tops during the growing season. Use affected roots as normal.

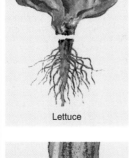

Lettuce

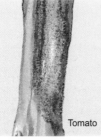

Tomato

GREY MOULD

Grey mould (**botrytis**) attacks plants through damaged areas and can spread to all the above-ground parts. Affected areas are usually brown and soft at first and then are covered with a grey or pale brown fluffy mould. Nearly all types of vegetables may be affected and it is encouraged by cool, wet and badly ventilated situations. On brassica leaves it often follows frost damage — on peas and beans the pods develop a velvety coating in wet weather. Infected lettuce plants turn reddish-brown at the base and may break off at stem level. Infected tomato stems bear grey furry patches and the fruit may show spots (**ghost spotting**) on the surface. The standard treatment is to remove diseased parts or whole plants and then spray the rest with carbendazim. Always remove decaying leaves, fruit etc to prevent infection.

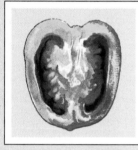

HALO BLIGHT

Small brown spots appear on the leaves of french and runner beans, each spot being surrounded by a yellow halo. Attacks are worst in wet weather and seedlings may be killed — plants which survive have disfigured pods. Destroy diseased plants. Do not sow blistered seed, do not soak before sowing and practise crop rotation.

HOLLOW FRUIT

Not a serious problem of tomatoes, but an indicator that something went wrong during the growing season. The usual cause is that conditions were poor for pollination — the air was too cold, too hot or too dry. Other possible reasons for air spaces in the fruit are too little potash in the soil or damage by a hormone weedkiller.

Spinach

Pea

LEAF SPOT

A number of different fungi can cause dark spots to appear on the leaves of vegetables. With beetroot, lettuce and spinach the spots are small and brown — the central area of each spot may drop out. The effect is unsightly but the result is not usually serious. **Leaf & pod spot** attacks peas — brown sunken spots appear on the pods and stems. Several leaf spot diseases attack brassicas — the usual one is **ring spot** which causes brown rings on the older leaves. For details of other leaf spot troubles see **celery leaf spot** (page 47), **chocolate spot** (page 47) and **anthracnose** (page 43). As a general rule leaf spots are encouraged by wet weather and overcrowding. Practise crop rotation — remove diseased parts and spray the crop with mancozeb. Lift and burn badly diseased plants.

LEEK MOTH

Pale green 1 cm grubs tunnel inside young onion and shallot leaves so that only the outer skin remains. Late attacks can be fatal. Leeks are the favourite host and here the pests burrow through the young leaves to produce a shot-hole effect as the foliage unfolds. Remove and burn badly affected leaves. Spray with bifenthrin.

MANGOLD FLY

Small white grubs of the mangold fly burrow inside the leaves of beetroot, producing blisters which turn brown and shrivel. Attacks occur from May onwards. Growth of young plants is retarded and their yield is reduced, but attacks on older plants have little effect. Remove damaged leaves — spray with a systemic insecticide.

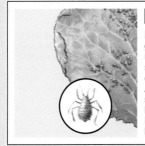

MEALY APHID

Large clusters of waxy, greyish greenflies can be found on the underside of leaves and on the stem tips of brassicas from June onwards in hot, dry weather. Affected leaves turn yellow — **sooty mould** may develop and brussels sprouts can be ruined. Not easy to control — spray with bifenthrin or pirimicarb.

MILLEPEDE

Black or spotted grubs which tend to curl up when disturbed. The underground parts of many vegetables are attacked, especially when the weather is cool and damp. Damaged or diseased areas are the prime targets. There are no control chemicals — destroy any millepedes you find when cultivating the soil.

NECK ROT

A storage disease of onions — greyish mould develops near the neck and the bulbs turn soft and rotten. Follow the rules for proper storage — dry the bulbs thoroughly and store only hard, undamaged ones in a cool place. Don't store bulbs with fleshy, green necks. Remove rotten bulbs. Treated seed is available.

NO FRUIT

A problem affecting several crops — flowers appear but do not set so that no fruit is produced. Tomato flowers sometimes wither and fall — this **blossom drop** is nearly always caused by dryness at the roots and in the air. Marrow flowers fail to set because pollination has not taken place — give nature a helping hand by dusting a male flower into the centre of several female ones. Flowering without pod production is a major problem with runner beans — possible causes include sparrow and bumble bee damage, cool weather at flowering time and dry soil at the roots.

NO HEARTS

A wide variety of factors can prevent lettuces from forming hearts. The most likely reason is shortage of organic matter — other possible causes are growing the plants in a shady site, severe aphid attack, overcrowding and drought. Brassicas have a number of related problems — cabbages may fail to heart, cauliflowers do not produce a head and sprouts are 'blown'. Once again too little organic matter is a possible cause, but the most likely reason for these brassica troubles is failing to plant firmly in well-consolidated soil. Other possibilities are drought, shade and lack of nutrients in the soil.

ONION FLY

The tell-tale sign of this onion pest is yellow drooping foliage. The 8 mm white maggots burrow into the base of the bulbs — young plants are frequently killed and older ones fail to develop properly. Attacks are worst in dry weather. Firm the soil around the plants — hoe regularly. Remove all thinnings from the site.

PARSNIP CANKER

The tops of parsnip roots become cracked and blackened — the tissues below may rot. A soil-borne fungus may be responsible, but this disease is usually linked with poor growing conditions, such as acid or starved soil and irregular rainfall. Don't sow too early. Next year choose a resistant variety such as Avonresister.

PEA & BEAN WEEVIL

The tell-tale sign is young foliage with U-shaped notches at the edges — the culprit is a 5 mm brown weevil. Seedlings can be killed but older plants usually quickly recover. There are hidden problems — adults carry viruses and the grubs eat root nodules. Hoe in spring. Spray with permethrin if necessary.

PEA MOTH

Maggoty peas are a familiar problem. The 8 mm greenish caterpillars burrow through the pods and into the peas, making them unusable. The best way to avoid trouble is to sow a quick-maturing variety either early or late in the season. Spraying with a contact insecticide 7-10 days after the start of flowering is less effective.

PEA THRIPS

These minute black or yellow insects are just visible. Silvery patches appear on the leaves and pods — yields are reduced. Attacks are worst in hot, dry weather. Water the plants during dry spells. An insecticide such as permethrin, heptenophos or horticultural soap can be used. Dig over after removing plants.

Potato

Tomato

POTATO BLIGHT

The first signs are brown patches on potato or tomato leaves — in damp weather each blight spot on the underside has a fringe of white mould. This disease can destroy all the foliage in a wet season. The disease does not travel down the stems to the tubers — the fungal spores are washed off the leaves and on to the soil by rain. If the tubers come into contact with live spores when harvesting then the tubers will develop blight in store. To prevent this from happening earth up the stems to keep the tubers covered and then cut off and remove all diseased growth 10 days before lifting. Infected tomatoes develop brown, sunken areas and soon rot. Spray potato plants with mancozeb in July — treat tomatoes as soon as they have been stopped. Repeat every 2 weeks if the weather is damp.

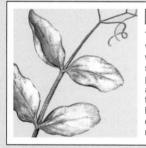

POWDERY MILDEW

The leaves and stems of several vegetables may be covered with white powdery patches of mildew spores during a warm, dry spell — peas, marrow, cucumber, turnip and swede are most at risk. Keep the soil moist — ventilate greenhouse crops. Spray with mancozeb and repeat every 2 weeks if necessary.

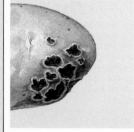

POWDERY SCAB

Powdery patches with raised edges occur on potato tubers — it is much less frequent than common scab (page 47) which has scurfy patches. Powdery scab is most severe in heavy soil under cool and wet conditions. It lasts in the soil for many years — avoid susceptible varieties such as Cara and Pentland Crown.

RED SPIDER MITE

A serious greenhouse pest which can attack beans outdoors when the weather is warm and dry. Silky webbing covers the leaves and stems. The foliage is bleached and speckled. Tiny mites (green in summer, red in winter) feed on the underside of the leaves. Maintain a damp atmosphere. Spray with bifenthrin or derris every 7 days.

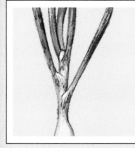

ROOT APHID

Lettuce, carrot, beans and parsnip can be attacked by this blue-green or grey aphid which feeds on the roots and causes white powdery patches on the root surface. Growth is stunted — leaves may turn yellow and wilt. You can water the surface with a greenfly killer but it is difficult to control. Practise crop rotation.

RUST

Rust is less of a problem with vegetables than in the flower garden. Leeks are the usual host — onions are occasionally infected. Orange spots and blotches appear on the surface of the leaves — unsightly, but the edible value is hardly affected. Do not grow leeks nor onions on land affected last year.

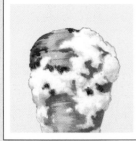

SCLEROTINIA ROT

White woolly mould covers the diseased tissues — black cyst-like bodies develop on this mould. It is the major disease of stored carrots, it attacks greenhouse cucumbers and occasionally appears on celery. Do not store soft carrots. Do not grow carrots, parsnips nor celery on infected land for 2 seasons.

SHANKING

The centre leaves of onions turn yellow and collapse — outer leaves soon follow. Evil-smelling slime develops within the scales. A destructive disease, but it is much less common than white rot (page 63). There is no practical method of prevention or treatment — do not grow onions nor shallots on infected ground for 5 years.

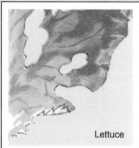

Lettuce

SLUGS & SNAILS

Generally regarded as enemy No.1 in the garden, especially when the weather is wet and cool. They are not usually seen during the day, so look for the tell-tale slime trails. Young plants are particularly susceptible and may be killed — the leaves of lettuce, brassicas, celery etc are holed and stems are damaged. Potato tubers may be riddled by the underground keeled slug. Keep the surrounding area free from rubbish. The standard method of control is to scatter slug pellets thinly around the plants at the first sign of attack. Non-chemical methods of killing or deterring slugs and snails are using traps filled with beer, placing a ring of gritty sand around individual plants and applying slug-killing nematodes to the soil. On heavy land avoid planting slug-susceptible potato varieties such as Cara and Maris Piper.

Potato

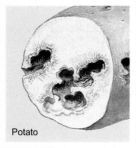

SMUT

A disease of leeks, onions and shallots. Grey streaks and spots appear on the stems and bulbs — these diseased areas burst to expose black powdery spores. Leaves become thickened and twisted. There is no treatment — lift and burn diseased plants. Do not grow leeks nor onions on infected land for at least 5 years.

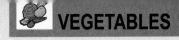

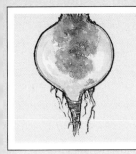

SOFT ROT

A slimy and evil-smelling bacterial rot which can affect growing plants such as turnips and swedes, but it is usually associated with badly stored bulbs and roots — potatoes, carrots, turnips, onions etc. The disease organisms enter through damaged tissues — take care when hoeing and store only firm and healthy vegetables.

SPLITTING

Carrot

Onion

Splitting is a common disorder of many vegetables. With some there is a simple cracking of the surface — commonly-seen examples are roots or tubers such as beetroots, carrots, swedes, turnips and potatoes. Other vegetables which may split are celery stalks, tomato fruits and cabbage hearts. In a few cases splitting is not obvious from the outside — **saddleback** of onions (splitting at the base) is seen when the outer layers are peeled away and **hollow heart** of potatoes is only apparent when the tuber is cut in two. Although splitting affects a variety of plants in a number of ways the cause is nearly always the same — heavy rain or watering after a prolonged period of drought. Never keep the plants short of water during dry spells. Use split potatoes, carrots etc as soon as possible as they will not keep in store.

STEM ROT

Stem rot (**didymella**) is a serious disease of tomatoes. Lower leaves turn yellow and a sunken brown canker appears at the base of the stem — black spots develop in the cankered area. Cucumbers are attacked by a closely-related fungus — leaves, stems and fruit are affected. Lift and burn infected plants. Good hygiene is essential.

SUN SCALD

A greenhouse tomato and cucumber problem. Papery patches appear on the leaf margins — brown depressions occur on the fruit. Exposure to bright sunshine is the cause, especially if the plant is wet. Apply shading. Do not spray at midday in sunny weather — leaves should be dry by nightfall if you water late in the day.

SWIFT MOTH

Soil-living white caterpillars — easy to recognise as they wriggle backwards when disturbed. The roots of lettuce and brassicas may be attacked — carrots and parsnips are hollowed out. There is no chemical control, but you can keep this pest in check by hoeing regularly and eradicating nearby weeds.

TIPBURN

The brown scorch at the edge of lettuce leaves is due to tipburn, sometimes called **greasiness**. It is not a disease — it is a disorder due to a sudden loss of water by the leaves. This can happen when there is a warm spell in early spring or at the start of a hot and dry spell in summer. There is no preventive measure.

TOMATO BUCKEYE ROT

A tomato disease which is caused by fungal spores being splashed up from the soil on to the lower trusses by either rain or watering. There are brown concentric rings around a grey spot on unripe fruit and a wet rot of the tissues below. Apply a peat mulch, water carefully and tie up the bottom trusses to reduce the risk of splashing.

TOMATO LEAF MOULD

This disease of greenhouse tomatoes is encouraged by night conditions which are too warm and too humid. It first appears on the lower leaves — purplish-brown mould patches on the underside and yellowish patches above. Remove diseased leaves and spray with carbendazim. Consider a resistant variety e.g Eurocross.

TOMATO MOTH

The young caterpillars eat holes in the leaves of greenhouse tomatoes — the mature caterpillars attack the developing fruits and render them unfit for eating. Look for the pests and remove them when perforated leaves or tunnelled fruit are seen. Spray with bifenthrin or fatty acids if this is not practical.

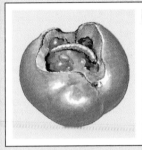

VERTICILLIUM WILT

A soil-borne disease which infects greenhouse tomatoes and cucumbers. The lower leaves turn yellow and wilt in hot weather but appear to recover on cool evenings. Brown streaks run through the stem tissue. Destroy badly diseased plants — mulch around the base of the others so new roots can form.

VIOLET ROOT ROT

The only above-ground symptom you will see is a slight yellowing of the foliage of carrots, parsnips, beetroots, turnips or swedes. On lifting, however, the harvested roots show a felt-like mass of purplish threads. Never store roots affected by violet root rot. Do not grow root crops nor asparagus on infected land for several seasons.

Cucumber mosaic virus

Potato leaf roll virus

Tomato fern-leaf virus

VIRUS

Virus diseases attack many vegetables and there is no cure. The main carriers are aphids, but there are other pests which take viruses from plant to plant — weevils, whiteflies, beetles etc. Infection may also be due to tools or hands which have touched diseased plants. There are numerous types — the most widespread are the **mosaic virus** diseases and the usual cause is the **cucumber mosaic virus**. Plants susceptible to attack by one or more of the mosaic viruses include marrows, cucumbers, beans, turnips, lettuces, potatoes and tomatoes. Affected leaves are mottled with yellow and dark green patches — the surface becomes puckered and distorted. The plants are severely stunted and may collapse. **Mottle virus** produces more diffuse patches of yellow than the mosaic viruses — carrots can be badly affected. Potatoes are the crop most likely to suffer from disease if virus-free seed is not used, and **leaf roll virus** is the one most likely to occur. **Tomato fern-leaf virus** is a common complaint of tomatoes — leaflets are extremely narrow. Tackling virus diseases involves several steps. Destroy badly infected plants. Buy virus-free seed or plants. Spray to control sap-sucking insects. Wash hands and tools after handling infected plants. Do not touch tomato plants after smoking.

WART DISEASE

A potato problem you will find in the textbooks but are hardly ever likely to see. Black warty outgrowths appear on the tubers — it was once a serious complaint but is now rare as nearly all modern varieties are immune. If it appears destroy the plants and inform the Ministry of Agriculture, Fisheries and Food.

WHITE BLISTER

White growths spread over the leaves of brassicas — growth is weakened and affected leaves may fall. Sprouts are more susceptible than other members of the cabbage family. Burn diseased foliage — thin out plants to reduce overcrowding. Do not plant brassicas on land which was affected in the previous season.

WHITE ROT

A serious disease of onions which is worst in hot, dry summers. A fluffy white mould in which small black fungal bodies are embedded grows on the base of the bulbs. The foliage turns yellow and wilts. There is no chemical treatment — lift and burn the diseased plants. Do not grow onions on infected land for at least 5 years.

WHITE TIP

A disease which occasionally attacks leeks in late summer or autumn. The leaf tips turn white and papery — the affected area starts to rot and moves downwards to ground level. Spray with carbendazim at the first signs of disease. Remove badly affected plants. Do not grow leeks on infected land for at least 2 years.

WHITEFLY

A troublesome pest of greenhouse vegetables such as tomatoes and cucumbers. Tiny moth-like insects feed on the underside of the foliage which becomes pale and curled. Hang yellow fly catcher cards above the plants. Outdoor crops can be affected when the weather is warm and dry — spray with bifenthrin.

WIRE STEM

A disease of brassica seedlings and young plants. The stem base becomes black and shrunken. As a result seedlings often die — the plants which survive grow slowly and their stems break easily. There is no treatment. Avoid growing seedlings in wet and cold soil or compost. Avoid overcrowding and overwatering.

WIREWORM

These pests can be a problem in new gardens and in plots adjoining grassland. They are slow moving — not active like the friendly centipede. Wireworms eat the roots of many vegetables and burrow into potato tubers. There is no chemical to use — good soil preparation and regular cultivation are the answer.

WITHERING

A disorder of greenhouse cucumbers. The fruits stop growing when only as long as a finger and withering spreads back from the tip. There are many possible causes such as draughts, the use of fresh manure etc but the most likely cause is faulty root action due to poor drainage, overwatering or poor soil preparation. The answer is to maintain steady growth by careful watering. If withering does take place remove the damaged fruit and for the next week withhold water — keep the floor damp as usual and ventilate the greenhouse. After this treatment resume watering and syringing as usual.

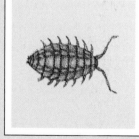

WOODLICE

A problem in greenhouses and gardens which are not properly cared for — woodlice hide under pots, old plants etc during the day and devour young leaves at night. They favour plants which have already been damaged. Control is not easy — remove garden rubbish and sprinkle bendiocarb dust around the plants.

CHAPTER 5

TREE FRUIT TROUBLES

APPLES

The major pests include aphids (especially on young trees) and caterpillars (especially winter moth). Codling moth is the main danger to developing fruit — in addition keep watch for apply sawfly and capsid. Scab and powdery mildew are the diseases you are most likely to see but you should also look out for canker and brown rot.

PEARS

As with apples both aphids and caterpillars are major pests. Pear and cherry slugworm can also be a serious nuisance and pear midge is an important cause of fruit drop. Among the major diseases are scab and the more deadly but less often seen fireblight.

PLUMS

Aphids are a major pest as with other tree fruit. Birds can seriously damage the flower buds and both wasps and plum sawfly can ruin the fruit. Watch for red spider mite in hot settled weather and look for the tell-tale signs of silver leaf, brown rot and bacterial canker.

CHERRIES

Aphid (cherry blackfly) can be devastating on these trees. Birds are another serious problem, attacking both flower buds and ripening fruit. As with plums both silver leaf and brown rot are important diseases and so is bacterial canker.

PEACHES

Aphids and red spider mites are important pests when the weather is hot and dry. There are several important diseases, including peach leaf curl, silver leaf, bacterial canker and split stone.

SPRAYING PROGRAMME

The usual control plan is to spray specific pests or diseases as they occur and at the times recommended on pages 67-75. This approach is recommended for the average gardener, but the really keen fruit grower often adopts a spray programme which is designed to provide blanket protection against the major and some of the minor troubles. Set out below is a typical spraying programme.

STAGE OF FRUIT DEVELOPMENT	SPRAY
BUD SWELLING	No need to spray
BUD BREAK	No need to spray
BUD BURST	Systemic fungicide
MOUSE EAR	No need to spray
GREEN CLUSTER	Systemic fungicide plus contact insecticide
PINK BUD (Apples) **WHITE BUD** (Pears)	Systemic fungicide
BLOSSOM TIME Early to mid May (Apples) Late April to early May (Pears)	DO NOT SPRAY
PETAL FALL When nearly all petals have fallen	Systemic fungicide plus systemic insecticide
FRUITLET Mid June	Systemic fungicide plus contact insecticide
FRUITLET Early July	Systemic fungicide plus contact insecticide

APHID

Several species of greenfly attack tree fruit — cherry foliage can be severely distorted by blackfly. The usual symptom of aphid infestation is curling of the young foliage — shoot growth is stunted and sticky honeydew coats young stems and leaves. Spray with bifenthrin at green cluster — repeat if necessary.

APPLE BLOSSOM WEEVIL

A pest of apples which may also affect pears. In spring the grubs feed inside the flower buds — the petals turn brown and fail to open. Inside you may find a white grub or the adult brown weevil. These weevils move on to the leaves where they feed. Spray with permethrin at green cluster if the problem was serious last year.

APPLE CANKER

The bark shrinks and cracks in concentric rings. A tell-tale sign is the presence of red growths in winter. A serious disease of apples and pears, especially on badly-drained soil. Cut off damaged twigs — cut out cankers from stems and branches and treat with a wound paint. Copper sprays at leaf fall help to prevent canker.

APPLE CAPSID

Reddish-brown spots on apple leaves expand to form ragged brown-edged holes. Damaged foliage is puckered and distorted — fruits develop corky patches on the surface. These 5 mm active insects are usually a minor pest which can be ignored, but use a fatty acid spray at green cluster if they are known to be troublesome.

APPLE SAWFLY

A ribbon-like scar is produced on the surface of the fruit. Later the grub burrows down to feed on the central core which causes the fruit to drop in June and July. The grubs go into the ground in July. Sticky frass can be seen around the hole. Spray with dimethoate at petal fall to prevent attack — burn all damaged apples.

APPLE SUCKER

The developing flower buds of apples and pears may be attacked by young apple suckers. The flowers turn brown as if attacked by frost, but careful examination reveals yellowish-white insects which look like flattened aphids. Another tell-tale sign is the presence of honeydew. Spray with bifenthrin at green cluster.

BACTERIAL CANKER

A serious disease of plums, cherries and other stone fruit. Pale-edged spots appear on the leaves — at a later stage gum oozes from the bark and affected branches die back. Tackle it promptly to save the tree. Cut out diseased branches and apply a wound paint. Apply a copper spray in August, September and October.

BITTER PIT

Small brown areas develop in surface tissue of apples, each one marked by a small depression in the skin. Brown bitter spots make the fruit inedible. It generally develops during storage and the causes are complex. Watering in summer is helpful — so is mulching but do not use straw. Avoid heavy pruning.

BLOSSOM WILT

In a mild, wet spring this disease can cause the blossom trusses of apples, pears and plums to wilt and turn brown — shoots are killed in a bad attack. Remove infected flowers and dead twigs in spring. In summer remove all fruit affected by brown rot (see below). A tar oil spray in January will reduce the risk of infection in spring.

BROWN ROT

Infected fruit turns brown and concentric rings of yellowish mould appear. Most tree fruit can be affected, but the disease is worst on apples. It is necessary to destroy diseased fruit as soon as it is seen on the tree or on the ground. Store only sound fruit and examine them at regular intervals. Spraying is not effective.

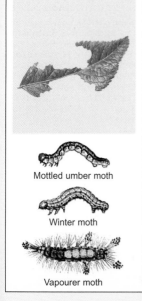

Mottled umber moth

Winter moth

Vapourer moth

CATERPILLAR

There are a number of caterpillars which eat the leaves of apples, pears, plums etc. The 2.5 cm colourful **vapourer moth** feeds on the foliage from May to August and the 5 cm black and yellow **buff-tip moth** can defoliate a young tree. The most important group are the 'looper' caterpillars which move with a looping action and may spin young leaves together. New foliage is devoured in spring and they then feed on the petals and flower stalks later in the season. All grow to about 3 cm but there are various colours. **March moth** is green with pale green stripes, **winter moth** is green and yellow, and the **mottled umber moth** is brown and yellow. Trees can be protected by encircling each trunk with a grease band — alternatively you can spray with bifenthrin before or after blossom time when the caterpillars are seen.

CODLING MOTH

The pale pink grub bores into developing fruit and feeds on the central core — the tell-tale sign of codling moth attack is sawdust-like frass. Apples are the main host but pears and plums may also be attacked. Grubs can be found inside the fruit in July and August. Spray with bifenthrin in mid June — repeat 3 weeks later.

CROWN GALL

Large, brown and warty out-growths sometimes occur on the stems and roots of fruit trees. Attacks are usually restricted to young trees on badly-drained sites. Mature trees are not harmed but newly-planted ones may lose vigour. Avoid planting in a badly-drained site. Galls can be cut off in autumn, but this is not necessary.

DIEBACK

The death of the stem begins at the tip and progresses slowly downwards — in time the tree may die. Dieback is more common on stone fruit than on apples and pears. Disease is the usual cause — look for fireblight, bacterial canker, honey fungus, phytoph-thora rot etc. Waterlogging is another reason for dieback.

FALSE SILVER LEAF

A common disorder which at first glance looks like silver leaf. The leaves are silvery but the effect appears all over the tree rather than moving progressively along the stem. A cut branch reveals that the staining associated with silver leaf is absent. The cause is irregular watering or nutrient defi-ciency. Mulch in spring.

FIREBLIGHT

A serious disease of pears which can occur on apples. Affected shoots wilt and die. Old cankers ooze in spring. The tell-tale sign is the presence of brown withered leaves which do not fall. Cut out affected branches to 60 cm below the brown leaves. Trees die when the trunk is infected — lift and burn.

FRUIT DROP

Fruitlets may drop after insect damage — look for grubs in fallen apples, pears and plums. Healthy fruitlets may also drop — this may be beneficial if there has been a heavy set. The first drop of apples takes place when the fruitlets are pea-sized but the major shedding of fruit is the June drop. It is normal for newly-planted trees to shed most of their fruit at this time and some varieties (e.g Cox's Orange Pippin) have a notoriously heavy June drop. If the number of fallen fruit is abnormally high for the variety and age of tree you should suspect starvation, irregular watering, frost damage or overcrowding.

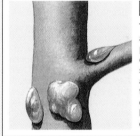

GUMMING

This disorder of cherries, plums and peaches usually occurs after a prolonged period of frost. Patches of gum on the branches and trunk set into hard lumps. This gum appears on healthy wood — with the more serious bacterial canker it oozes through diseased bark. Poor soil conditions are the cause.

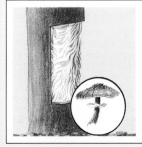

HONEY FUNGUS

Honey fungus is a common cause of the death of apple trees. A white fan of fungal growth occurs below the bark near ground level. On roots black 'bootlaces' are found. Toadstools appear in autumn at the base. Burn diseased stems and roots of diseased trees. A phenolic soil drench may reduce spread but control is difficult.

NO FRUIT

It is annoying when a tree which was full of blossom loses its flowers without setting fruit. If it is an annual event the most likely cause is the absence of a pollination partner. If it is not usual then blossom wilt can be the cause, but it is more probably due to frost damage, very dry air or a cold and wet spring.

PEACH LEAF CURL

The leaves of peaches and apricots develop large red blisters — the tree is weakened and early leaf fall occurs. The fungus overwinters in the bark and between bud scales, not on fallen leaves. It is a serious disease which deserves treatment. Spray with mancozeb in mid February, 2 weeks later and again at leaf fall.

PEAR/CHERRY SLUGWORM

These slimy, slug-like insects are the larval stage of the pear and cherry sawfly — they attack the leaves of pears, cherries, apples and plums between June and October. The slugworm feeds on the upper surface of the leaf, producing irregular shaped papery windows. Spray with a contact insecticide if the attack is severe.

PEAR LEAF BLISTER MITE

A serious pest of pears grown against walls. The microscopic mites cause pale green pimples in spring which later change to red and then black blisters. The damaged leaves fall early and fruit may be blistered. Insecticides are not effective — pick off and burn blistered leaves as soon as they are noticed.

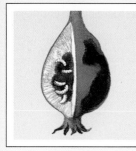

PEAR MIDGE

A serious pear pest. Fruitlets which have been attacked start to turn black a few weeks after petal fall and usually drop from the tree. Inside the fallen fruit there is a large cavity in which there are numerous 3 mm pale buff grubs. Pick and burn blackened fruit and keep the soil around the trunk well cultivated.

PEAR STONY PIT

This virus disease of pears is dangerous — affected trees have to be dug up and destroyed. Diseased fruits are small and mis-shapen with the surface covered with dimples and lumps. The flesh is woody and inedible. It usually occurs on old trees and it can spread to surrounding pears. Always buy virus-free stock.

PLUM SAWFLY

The tell-tale sign of this serious pest of plums is a hole surrounded by black sticky frass on the surface of the fruit. Inside can be found the 1 cm creamy-white grub of the plum sawfly. Damaged fruits fall to the ground before maturity. Culti-vate the soil around the trees. Dimethoate can be sprayed 7 days before petal fall to prevent attack.

POWDERY MILDEW

A major disease of apples which may also attack pears — young leaves, shoots and flower trusses are covered with greyish-white mould in spring. Growth is stunted, leaves may fall and fruit may fail to set. Remove infected twigs. For chemical control use a programme containing carbendazim — see page 66.

RED SPIDER MITE

The first sign of attack on apples and plums is a faint mottling of the upper leaf surface. In warm, dry weather the infestation may be severe — the leaves turn bronze, become brittle and die. Look for the tiny mites on the underside of the leaves. Spray with bifenthrin in late May and repeat if necessary 3 weeks later.

RUSSETTING

Russetting is the rough scurf which sometimes forms over the surface of apples and pears. On some apples it is a natural feature of the variety — on the smooth-skinned varieties it is an unsightly disorder, but the eating quality is not affected. Possible causes are poor weather at petal fall, drought, powdery mildew or nutrient shortage.

SCAB

A serious disease of apples and pears — leaves are spotted, twigs are blistered and the dark-coloured scabs on young fruit develop into large corky areas. Attacks are worst in warm, damp weather. For chemical control use a spraying programme containing carbendazim. Alternatively spray as recommended with mancozeb.

SHOT HOLE DISEASE

A fungal disease which affects plums, peaches and cherries. Brown spots appear on the leaves — as the foliage expands these brown areas fall out and are replaced by round holes scattered over the surface. Trees weakened by poor growing conditions are favoured — the answer is to water, feed and mulch properly.

SILVER LEAF

The most serious disease of plums which can also affect apples, cherries and peaches. The spores enter through a wound, and the first sign is silvering of the leaves. Dieback occurs and the wood is stained. Cut out dead branches before July to 15 cm below the infection — dig out bracket toadstools if they appear on the bark.

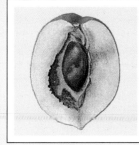

SPLIT STONE

An affected peach is holed at the stalk end and inside the stone is split and rotten. The cause may be poor pollination — next year hand pollinate and gently mist the blossom in dry weather. Lack of lime may be responsible, but the most likely cause is irregular watering. Muloh in spring and water during prolonged dry weather.

WASP

All types of fruit may be attacked by wasps. Soft-skinned types such as plums are favoured and may be completely devoured. Apples and pears usually escape if the surface is undamaged. Spraying is not effective — the answer is to find the nest and destroy it with a chemical wasp-killer. Do this job at dusk.

WOOLLY APHID

Colonies of aphids secrete a white waxy coating which protects them from other creatures. Their presence does little direct harm, but the corky galls they produce are an entry point for canker spores. You can apply a drenching spray of bifenthrin but it is usually easier to paint the solution on with an old toothbrush.

CHAPTER 6

SOFT FRUIT TROUBLES

STRAWBERRIES

The three major pests are aphid, birds and slugs — spider mite and tortrix moth can also be a problem. The important diseases are grey mould, strawberry mildew and virus.

RASPBERRIES

The major pests include aphid, raspberry beetle, raspberry moth and birds. Mosaic virus is a serious disease carried by aphids — other major diseases are cane spot, spur blight and grey mould.

BLACKCURRANTS

Aphids and birds are major pests as with most types of soft fruit — big bud mite, gall midge and spider mite are also important. Major diseases include reversion virus, american mildew, grey mould and leaf spot.

BLACKBERRIES

Aphids, capsid bug, birds and raspberry beetle can all be serious pests — the diseases to watch for are cane spot, spur blight, grey mould and rust.

GOOSEBERRIES

The pests to watch for are aphids, gooseberry sawfly, magpie moth and birds. The important diseases are american mildew, dieback, leaf spot and cluster cup rust.

GRAPES

The range of major insect pests is small — scale (see page 36) and spider mite are the only ones you are likely to see. Major diseases include vine mildew and grey mould. Shanking is an important disorder.

AMERICAN MILDEW

A crippling disease of gooseberries which appears on the young leaves and later on the fruits as a white mould which changes to brown. It is encouraged by overcrowding. Cut out diseased branches in September — next year spray with carbendazim when first flowers open and repeat twice at 2 week intervals.

APHID

Blister aphid

Leaf-curling aphid

Numerous types of aphid attack soft fruit and the damage they do can be serious. In some cases there is severe leaf distortion, but the main danger is usually due to the viruses they carry. Currants are attacked by **currant blister aphid** which produces coloured blisters on the leaves. Both **lettuce aphid** and **gooseberry aphid** cause severe leaf curling on gooseberries. Two aphid species attack raspberries — the **rubus aphid** and the stem-coating **raspberry aphid**. Strawberries can be invaded by other species — the **strawberry aphid** and the more serious **shallot aphid** which can cripple the plant. A winter spray on cane and bush fruit will kill the eggs of these pests but the usual treatment is to apply a contact insecticide such as bifenthrin when the pests appear and then repeat the spray as recommended.

BIG BUD MITE

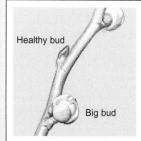

Healthy bud

Big bud

The tell-tale sign is the presence of winter buds which are swollen and less pointed than normal — in spring these infested buds fail to open. The microscopic mites enter the buds in summer — they are carriers of the reversion virus (page 81). Pick off enlarged buds in winter — dig up and burn badly infested plants.

BLOSSOM WEEVIL

Strawberries and raspberries can be attacked — the flower stalk is partially severed by the adult weevil after eggs have been laid inside the flower bud. The grubs develop inside the damaged bud which withers and may fall. Similar to strawberry rhynchites but colour is different — blossom weevil is greyish black.

CANE SPOT

In early summer small purple spots appear on raspberry and loganberry canes — these spots increase in size to form shallow white pits with purple borders. Canes may be killed. Cut out badly diseased canes in autumn. Next spring spray with carbendazim at 2 week intervals from bud burst until blossom appears.

CAPSID BUG

All types are attacked, especially currants and gooseberries. Small bugs puncture the leaf surface, producing brown spots. As the leaves expand these spots turn into ragged brown-edged holes. Not easy to control — if the trouble occurs each year apply a fatty acid spray when first flowers open and again at fruit set.

CLEARWING MOTH

Dead or dying shoots of currants or gooseberries may indicate that the 1.5 cm white caterpillars of this moth are present. The eggs are laid in June and after hatching the caterpillars tunnel into the pith of the shoots where they feed. It is not a widespread pest — cut back affected shoots to where the pith is healthy.

CLUSTER CUP RUST

Several rust diseases affect soft fruit (**raspberry rust**, **blackberry rust** etc) but they are rarely serious. Cluster cup rust is a gooseberry disease — yellow-edged pits appear on the orange-coloured diseased patches. It only appears where sedges are growing nearby. Spray if necessary with mancozeb before flowering.

EELWORM

Strawberry is the crop most likely to suffer and there are several different eelworms which may be responsible. Leaf stalks may be abnormally long and turn red (**red plant disease**) or leaf and flower stalks may be abnormally short and thickened. Dig up and burn badly infested plants — do not replant for at least 5 years.

GALL MIDGE

The gall midge or **leaf midge** is a serious pest of blackcurrants. The small maggots at the shoot tips cause the young foliage to become twisted, distorted and discoloured — these leaves usually turn black as they develop. Affected shoots may die. It is not easy to control — spray with a systemic insecticide as soon as damage is first noticed.

GOOSEBERRY SAWFLY

This 2.5 cm spotted caterpillar is a serious pest of gooseberries and currants — a bush can be completely defoliated in a few days. Keep careful watch from May onwards — the caterpillars feed at the edges of the leaf tissue. Spray with a contact insecticide such as bifenthrin — a second spray may be necessary.

GREY MOULD

This fluffy mould is destructive to raspberries, strawberries, currants and grapes in a wet summer — the fungus usually enters through wounds caused by pests such as slugs. Remove mouldy plant material immediately. Prevent attacks by spraying with carbendazim when first flowers open and repeat after petal fall.

LEAF SPOT

An important disease of blackcurrants — gooseberries may also be attacked. Brown spots appear and early leaf fall takes place. Remove diseased leaves. Prevent attacks by spraying with carbendazim at the first sign of disease and repeat every 2 weeks if necessary. Strawberry leaf spot rarely warrants spraying.

MAGPIE MOTH

This brightly-coloured looper caterpillar can seriously defoliate gooseberries and currants in spring and early summer but it is no longer a common pest. Hand picking will usually give satisfactory control. A heavy infestation calls for spraying with a contact insecticide such as bifenthrin when the first flowers are about to open.

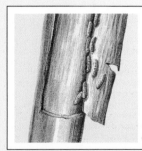

MIDGE BLIGHT

Maggots of **raspberry cane midge** feed under the bark of young canes. Direct injury is slight, but the damaged tissue is attacked by **cane blight** which causes the canes to snap off at ground level — this insect/disease complex is known as midge blight. Cut off diseased canes — spray young stems with bifenthrin.

NO FRUIT

If the plants are healthy and not suffering from water shortage at the roots then there are two basic causes for the failure of fruit to set. Either frost occurred when the bushes or canes were in flower or pollination was defective due to poor weather which inhibited insect activity. Very dry air at blossom time can also be a factor.

RASPBERRY BEETLE

The most serious pest of raspberries, loganberries and blackberries — the adult beetles feed on the flowers and the grubs bore inside the fruits where they feed. Use bifenthrin — spray raspberries when the first fruits turn pink. Spray loganberries when the petals have fallen and blackberries just before the first flowers open.

RASPBERRY MOTH

Dead or dying shoots of raspberries may indicate that the 1 cm red caterpillars of the raspberry moth are present. The young caterpillars live in the soil in winter and move to the shoots in April, where they bore into and feed on the pith. A winter tar oil spray will kill the hibernating caterpillars. Cut out and burn withered shoots.

Healthy   Reverted

REVERSION

This virus disease of blackcurrants changes the leaf shape. The cleft at the base disappears and the main lobe has less than 10 serrations. A simpler symptom to spot is the presence of red rather than grey flower buds. The virus is spread by the big bud mite. Destroy diseased plants — plant certified stock on a fresh site.

ROOT DEATH

There are several diseases and pests which can kill the roots of strawberries. Diseases include **red core** which can be recognised by the red colour of the inner tissues of the dead roots. **Black root rot** results in blackened decaying roots and **verticillium wilt** causes wilting before root death. There is no cure — destroy the plants and grow a different crop on the site. Some general pests dealt with elsewhere eat the roots of strawberries — see **cutworm** (page 11) and **swift moth** (page 18). **Strawberry root weevil** grubs feed on the roots from autumn to spring. Nematode-based biological controls are available.

RUST

Several rust diseases affect soft fruit — examples are **cluster cup rust** on gooseberries (page 79), **raspberry rust**, **blackberry rust** and **white pine rust** on blackcurrant (illustrated). Remove stems which are badly diseased. To prevent rust apply mancozeb in spring and repeat every 2 weeks, but it is rarely worthwhile.

SEED BEETLE

These insects attack strawberries — the seeds and the attached flesh are eaten so that the fruits are badly disfigured. The 1 cm black beetles are very active and move on to the crop from surrounding weeds where they feed. Keep the strawberry bed free from weeds and dead leaves. Rather similar damage is caused by birds.

SHANKING

The fruit stalks shrivel and there is an overall shrinkage of grapes — the colour is poor and the taste is sour. Possible causes are over-cropping, underwatering and waterlogging. Shrinkage due to **sun scald** occurs only at the top of the fruit and the stalks do not shrivel — shade the greenhouse and ventilate in sunny weather.

SLUGS & SNAILS

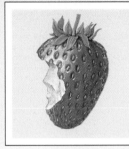

A large hole eaten in the side of a strawberry is usually due to slugs and snails (look for slime trails) or the strawberry ground beetle. Gooseberries, currants and raspberries are less seriously affected. Keep the area free from dead leaves and rubbish. The standard method of control is to scatter slug pellets thinly around the plants.

SPIDER MITE

Strawberry mite

Several types attack soft fruit — **red spider mite**, **bryobia mite**, **strawberry mite** etc. The general symptoms are bronze-coloured leaves and the presence of minute mites on the undersurface. Some but not all can be kept in check by spraying with derris every 3 weeks — the strawberry mite is not controlled by spraying.

SPUR BLIGHT

Purplish patches appear around the buds on raspberry and loganberry canes in early autumn. These patches turn silvery and the buds are killed. Reduce overcrowding. Cut out diseased canes when purple patches appear. Prevent attacks by spraying with carbendazim every 2 weeks from bud burst to the start of flowering.

STRAWBERRY MILDEW

This powdery mildew is easy to recognise. Dark patches appear on the upper surface of the leaves — the infected foliage curls upwards to expose greyish mould patches. Diseased fruits are dull and shrivelled. Spray with carbendazim at the start of flowering and again 2 weeks later. Cut off and burn leaves after harvesting.

STRAWBERRY RHYNCHITES

The stalks of strawberry and raspberry blossom trusses are punctured by this pest in May and June. The unopened buds wither and may fall. Do not confuse with blossom weevil damage — strawberry rhynchites has a greenish metallic body. Damage is rarely serious — if necessary spray with a contact insecticide.

TORTRIX MOTH

The strawberry tortrix moth can be a serious pest. Several leaves are joined together by silken threads — the 5 mm green caterpillars feed inside this protective cover. Fruits are occasionally attacked. These spun leaves should be picked off. If spraying is necessary apply bifenthrin before flowering and repeat after picking.

Dieback

TREE & SHRUB TROUBLES

Some of the diseases and pests which attack a wide range of shrubs, trees and/or fruit trees may damage soft fruit. Examples are leaf-eating **caterpillars** (pages 27 and 69), **crown gall** (page 70), **dieback** (page 70), **honey fungus** (page 71), **silver leaf** (page 75), **wasps** (page 75) and **coral spot** (page 28).

VINE MILDEW

This powdery mildew is common on both outdoor and greenhouse grapes. White patches appear on the leaves — the fruit is covered with powdery mould and splitting may take place. Burn diseased leaves and prune thoroughly in autumn. Apply carbendazim when the disease is first seen — repeat every 2 weeks if necessary.

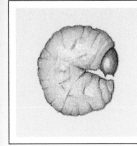

VINE WEEVIL

The curled wrinkled grubs of the vine weevil have become a serious menace to pot plants. Attacks are less frequent in the garden but the roots of raspberries, strawberries, gooseberries and vines may be eaten between autumn and spring. There is no simple chemical treatment but biological control products are available.

Mosaic

Yellow edge

VIRUS

Virus diseases are a major problem of raspberries and strawberries. Other soft fruit types are less affected although the reversion virus (page 81) is a serious complaint of blackcurrants. Aphids are the major carriers. **Mosaic** is the most damaging virus disease of raspberries — yellow patches appear on the distorted leaves and yields are reduced. Do not confuse with the yellow patches caused by the **leaf and bud mite** which is harmless. Strawberries are susceptible to several viruses — **crinkle** occurs in late spring, **yellow edge** in autumn and **arabis mosaic** in spring or autumn. Always buy plants which are certified as virus-free and look for aphid-resistant varieties. Remove and burn infected plants — grow replacement stock on a fresh site. Do not propagate from infected plants.

YELLOW-TAIL MOTH

A hairy caterpillar which can cause partial skeletonization of raspberry leaves. Attacks are generally light as these colourful 3 cm insects do not form colonies. This means that spraying with bifenthrin is not usually necessary. Pick off the caterpillars by hand but be careful — the bristles can produce a skin rash if you do not wear gloves.

CHAPTER 7

LAWN TROUBLES

DEALING WITH PROBLEMS

Earthworms, leatherjackets and moles are the major pests and their control is not easy. Chemicals to kill earthworms and leatherjackets are no longer available, and the poison used by mole catchers is far too toxic for amateur use. Brown patches caused by bitch or rabbit urine are another problem you may have to put up with if you are a dog owner or live in a rural area.

Diseases are less widespread than the major pests but they can be even more dangerous. Some like red thread are merely unsightly but ophiobolus patch can be a killer. Take remedial action as soon as the first patches have been identified — carbendazim is the fungicide to use. Unfortunately there is no fungicide to eradicate fairy rings.

Brown patches during prolonged dry weather are the most common lawn disorder. When deciding whether to water or not do remember that lawns recover when the rains return but newly-planted shrubs, herbaceous border perennials and bedding plants do not. There is a loss of quality, however, so water a luxury lawn if you can.

PREVENTING PROBLEMS

Prevention is better than cure is a maxim which applies to problems all round the garden, but it is especially important for the lawn. The reasons are that most lawn problems are difficult or impossible to control, and if something goes wrong you cannot simply dig it out and replace it with something else.

• **RAKE GENTLY IN SPRING AND AUTUMN** Use a spring-tine rake to remove surface rubbish and reduce build-up of thatch. Do not rake heavily in spring.

• **MOW REGULARLY** Timing and height of cut depend on your lawn type. As a general rule start in March and finish in October. In summer set the cut at 3 cm for ordinary turf or 1.5 cm for fine-grass turf. See The Lawn Expert for more details. Make sure the blades are sharp and set properly.

• **FEED** Apply a nitrogen-rich fertilizer in late spring.

• **KILL WEEDS AND MOSS WHEN THEY APPEAR** Don't wait until the problem gets out of hand — see Chapters 12 and 13.

• **WATER A LUXURY LAWN BEFORE IT STARTS TO GO BROWN** Begin 7-10 days after the start of a dry spell.

For the showpiece lawn there are additional tasks such as scarifying in autumn and brushing in a top dressing (peat or peat substitute, loam and coarse sand) to improve grass vigour and fill in minor hollows.

ALGAE

A coating of green or black slime which indicates poor drainage — it is encouraged by overrolling, underfeeding and mowing too closely. Algal growth is common under the drip-line of trees. Ferrous sulphate and dichlorophen will kill algae, but the basic cause must be removed to prevent its return. Spike and top dress in autumn.

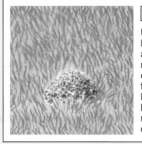

ANT

Unlike worm casts the hills made by ants are a feature of sandy soil and dry summer weather. They are not as harmful as the casts of earthworms but the hills can disfigure the surface if they occur in large numbers. Scatter with a besom before mowing — if numerous sprinkle an ant-killer over the affected area.

BITCH URINE

Bitch urine has a scorching effect on turf — the brown patches are roughly circular with a ring of dark lush grass around each one. The effect is worst in dry weather. There are no effective repellents to safeguard the whole lawn — the only thing you can do is to water the patches copiously. Reseed or returf if it is too unsightly.

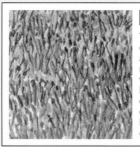

BROWN TIPPING

There are a number of possible causes for the browning of cut tips after mowing. The most likely reason is using a rotary mower with dull blades — the grass is bruised instead of being cut cleanly. With a cylinder mower check the setting and inspect the bottom plate for damage. Another cause is mowing wet grass.

CHAFER GRUB

The curved grubs of the garden chafer gnaw at the roots in spring and summer — small brown patches of grass appear which can be pulled away quite easily. They are less troublesome than leatherjackets and control measures are rarely needed. In sandy soil they can be a nuisance — rolling in spring will crush the grubs.

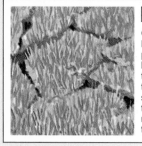

CRACKING

Cracks on the surface are due to lack of water — a common problem on April-sown lawns on heavy land. Water the whole lawn, top dress the cracked area and then sow a thin sprinkling of grass seed. It is much better to avoid trouble by remembering to water a new lawn in dry weather so that the soil does not dry out.

DOLLAR SPOT

A disease of fine-leaved grasses such as creeping red fescue and cumberland turf. The straw-coloured patches are circular and 2.5-5 cm wide — they may join together and badly disfigure the lawn. Feed with a nitrogen-rich fertilizer in spring and spike the turf in autumn. Apply carbendazim when the first patches are seen.

EARTHWORM

Worm casts render the surface uneven and stifle fine grasses. The cast-forming species of earthworms are not efficient soil aerators, and they do attract moles. There are no chemicals to use these days — all you can do is to scatter the dry casts before mowing, remove clippings when mowing and apply lawn sand in spring.

FAIRY RING

A ring of toadstools which grows wider each year. The worst is produced by Marasmius — two dark green circles with a bare space between. The slender brown-capped toadstools are 5-10 cm high. Many cures have been proposed over the years but replacing the soil and returfing is the only satisfactory answer.

FERTILIZER SCORCH

Overdosing is usually due to careless spreading by hand or by overlapping when a fertilizer distributor is used. The effect is either dark green or brown patches or stripes depending on the material and the degree of overdosing. The grass should recover in a few weeks — to speed up this recovery water the affected area copiously.

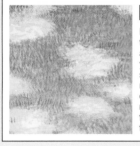

FUSARIUM PATCH

Fusarium patch (**snow mould**) is the most common lawn disease. In autumn or spring round patches of yellowing grass appear which spread to about 30 cm across and may merge. In damp weather the edges are covered with white mould. Do not use a nitrogen-rich fertilizer in autumn. The standard treatment is carbendazim.

LEATHERJACKET

The worst of all insect pests, especially in heavy soil after a wet autumn. The 3 cm brown grubs devour roots and stem bases in spring — the grass turns yellow or brown. There is no chemical treatment. Water in the evening and spread a plastic sheet over the surface. Remove next morning and brush away the grubs.

LICHEN

The upper surface of each leaf-like plate is nearly black when moist — the surface colour fades when dry and the edges curl upwards. Like moss it indicates poor growing conditions — too much shade, too little food and/or poor drainage. Lawn sand will kill it, but removal of the cause is the only way to prevent lichen from returning.

MINING BEE

This stingless bee makes its nest below the surface. The excavated soil is deposited as a small conical mound — at first glance it looks like an anthill, but there is a tell-tale crater at the top. Mining bees can be killed with derris but they are useful pollinators and so it is much better to just scatter the hills before mowing.

MOLE

Mole activity can destroy the even surface of the lawn. Large heaps of earth suddenly appear — attacks are most likely in sandy soil and lawns which receive little traffic. Remove the hills before mowing. Many remedies have been recommended but only traps offer long-term success. Employ a professional mole catcher if you can.

OPHIOBOLUS PATCH

It begins as a small sunken area which increases in size until it is a metre or more across. The edge is bleached and the central dead area is colonised by weeds and coarse grasses. Ophiobolus patch is often a feature of poor drainage, underfeeding and/or overliming — fortunately it is not common. Returf while the patch is still small.

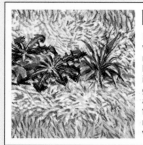

RED THREAD

Red thread (**corticium disease**) appears as irregular patches of bleached grass in late summer or autumn — these patches develop a pinkish tinge. Look closely in moist weather and you will find red needle-like growths on the leaves. This disease is a feature of starved lawns — feed in spring. Unsightly, but not fatal.

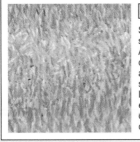

SCALPING

Scalping is all too familiar — high spots shaved bare by the mower. A cylinder mower is more likely to cause scalping than a rotary model and control calls for several measures. Raise the height of cut if the lawn is bumpy and improve the evenness of the surface by top dressing. Do not press downwards on the handle when mowing.

SPILT OIL

Spilt oil produces an irregular brown patch on the lawn which may eventually die. It appears suddenly a few days after mowing and is due to refuelling or oiling while the mower is standing on the lawn. Obviously the mower should be moved off the lawn before adding oil or filling with petrol. Returf the patch if necessary.

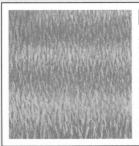

WASHBOARDING

A series of broad and regular corrugations about 15-30 cm apart run cross-wise along the mown strip. It is caused by always mowing in the same direction — this sets up a vibration pattern which eventually produces a ripple effect in the soil. The answer is simple — change the direction of the cut occasionally when you mow.

CHAPTER 8

ANIMAL PESTS

BIRDS

The flower garden is least affected — only crocus, polyanthus and Primula wanda are stripped of buds and flowers. Vegetables can suffer badly, especially peas and brassicas. Seed and seedlings are eaten, sparrows tear flowers and pigeons strip away the soft portion of leaves (illustrated). Flowers of forsythia and some other shrubs may be stripped but it is the fruit garden which suffers most of all. Bullfinches (illustrated) and sparrows devour buds of cherries, gooseberries etc — ripening fruit is also attacked. Small areas can be protected with soft plastic netting — secure the base properly. For a larger number of plants a fruit cage is the answer. Spray-on repellents are of limited value and are removed by rain. Mechanical scarers may be effective at first but they can lose their ability to frighten away birds.

A number of animals can cause damage, but the approach to them must be different to the way we tackle insect pests. The object must be to protect the plants and/or discourage the invaders without harming them — the fruit cage above is an example. There are exceptions — rats must be killed and moles too, if all else fails.

CATS

Cats are a pest in the garden — seed beds and transplants are disturbed by their scratching and young trees may be damaged by their claws. Protection is not easy if a cat has chosen your vegetable plot as a toilet. You can try one of the newer cat repellent sprays or a sonic deterrent but there is no fool-proof method.

DEER

Deer can be a menace in rural areas close to woodland. Woody shoots are severed and bark may be rubbed away — rose buds are a favourite meal. Fencing at least 2 m high is the best answer but this may not be practical. The trunks of trees can be protected with fine-mesh wire netting — deterrent sprays have limited value.

DOGS

Dogs, like cats, will disturb ground where plants are growing but the serious effect is the scorch caused by their urine. Conifers etc are damaged by dogs — lawns are disfigured by bitches. Copiously water the area as soon as you can but there is no satisfactory answer. The effect of deterrent dusts and sprays is short-lived.

FOXES

Foxes can be a nuisance in both town and country gardens. Dustbins are knocked over, plants are dug up and shrubs are scorched by their urine. There is no way of keeping foxes out of the average garden and there is no way of protecting the plants — conifers are especially vulnerable. Deterrents are of little value.

MICE & RATS

Mice will dig for planted peas, sweet corn, crocus corms etc — whole rows of large seeds may be removed. Between spring and autumn they will come indoors to attack stored fruit and vegetables. Proprietary mouse baits are available — mouse traps require some form of pet protection. Contact the council if rats are discovered.

MOLES

The tunnelling by moles can cause root damage and their hills are unsightly — a serious invasion can ruin a lawn. Unlike rabbits these pests are solitary creatures but the few which are present are difficult to eradicate. Try the simple ways first — smokes, sonic deterrents etc but call in a professional exterminator if all else fails.

RABBITS

A serious problem in rural areas — flowers and vegetables are nibbled, shrubs are attacked and tree bark may be gnawed in winter. Rabbit urine causes brown patches in the lawn. There is no easy answer — deterrents soon lose their power and ordinary fences are ineffective. Tree guards will protect individual plants.

SQUIRRELS

Nice to watch, but they can be a nuisance and their damage is often blamed on rabbits. They eat bulbs, nibble shoot tips, remove flower buds, carry away soft fruit and strip the bark off trees. As with rabbits there is no simple solution. Secure net-covered cages for groups of plants and individual tree guards are the only sure protection.

CHAPTER 9

GENERAL DISORDERS

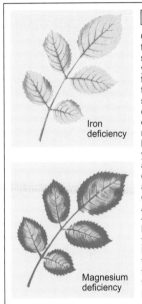

Iron deficiency

Magnesium deficiency

CHLOROSIS

Chlorosis is the yellowing of leaf tissues. It is natural for an occasional tree or shrub leaf to turn yellow, but when most or all of the foliage changes in this way during the active growing season then something is wrong. The most common reason is **lime-induced chlorosis** — many shrubs such as rhododendron, camellia and hydrangea develop pale green or yellow leaves when grown in alkaline soil. The cause is **iron deficiency** (young leaves worst affected) or **manganese deficiency** (old leaves worst affected). Add peat to the soil when planting — apply a chelated compound. **Magnesium deficiency** causes yellowing at the centre and early leaf fall. Red tints develop between the veins — apply a fertilizer containing magnesium. Chlorosis of the lower leaves is often due to poor drainage.

Not all troubles are caused by pests and diseases — split tomatoes and frost-damaged pear blossom (illustrated above) may not appear in plant trouble charts but they are still important problems. These two troubles are specific to a group of plants but there are disorders which can affect nearly the whole garden and these are described here. Disorders are due to faults in cultivation or an adverse environment.

COLD DAMAGE

A sudden cold snap in spring can affect developing leaves and buds of many herbaceous perennials, annuals and bulbs by destroying chlorophyll. The affected leaf, when it expands, may be yellow-edged (anemone, sweet pea etc), almost white (many bedding plants) or white-banded (narcissus). Pick off badly affected leaves.

DROUGHT

Dryness at the roots is the commonest cause of plant death. With woody plants the first sign is wilting of the foliage and in the early stage the effect is reversible. The next stage is browning of the foliage and then leaf drop which is extremely serious or fatal. Water before symptoms appear — mulch around plants.

Rose

Apple

FROST

With non-hardy plants frost threatens life itself — it is essential to wait until the danger of frost is over before sowing or transplanting. A hard frost can damage the tender new growth of hardy plants such as potatoes, roses, apples etc. The affected leaves may be bleached, blistered, cracked or scorched along the margins. The stems of early potatoes may be blackened — the crop can be protected by covering with newspaper if frosts are expected. The worst effects of frost are seen in the fruit garden. Frost at blossom time can cause the blossom of tree fruit to turn brown and drop off. With cane fruit some or all the buds may fail to open in the spring. The damage usually occurs when frost follows an unusually mild spell at the time when the buds are about to burst. To protect shrubs etc use horticultural fleece over the stems.

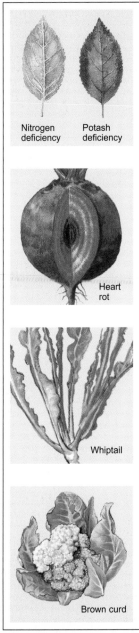

Nitrogen deficiency Potash deficiency

Heart rot

Whiptail

Brown curd

NUTRIENT SHORTAGE

Some minerals are required by the plant in quite large quantities — these major nutrients include nitrogen, phosphorus, potassium, calcium and magnesium. Others are needed in only small amounts — these trace elements include iron, boron, manganese, copper, zinc and molybdenum. Trees and shrubs growing in the open garden are unlikely to show symptoms of nutrient shortage unless you are growing a lime-hating variety in alkaline soil — see page 95. On the other hand fruit, vegetables, roses and flowers may show deficiency symptoms.

LEAF SYMPTOMS
Nitrogen deficiency produces young leaves which are pale and undersized — with some plants such as roses the mature foliage develops red spots or all-over red or yellow tinto. **Potash deficiency** results in brown brittle margins and downward-turning tips. With **manganese deficiency** there is browning between the veins — it is often associated with the use of high-potash fertilizers.

NON-LEAF SYMPTOMS
A number of vegetable disorders are due to nutrient shortage:
Marsh spot — peas. Brown-lined cavity in the centre of each pea due to manganese deficiency. **Heart rot** — beetroot. Blackened area within the flesh due to boron deficiency. **Speckled yellows** — beetroot. Rolled leaves, yellow patches between the veins due to manganese deficiency. **Whiptail** — cauliflower. Thin, strap-like leaves due to molybdenum deficiency. **Brown curd** — cauliflower. Discoloured heads due to boron deficiency. **Blossom end rot** — tomatoes. Leathery patch at base due to calcium deficiency.

Prevention and treatment measures include feeding with a compound fertilizer and mulching with compost or old manure each spring — use a product which contains the deficient element.

POOR PLANTING DAMAGE

Poor planting is one of the commonest causes of poor growth or death of trees and shrubs which have been grown in containers. Matted roots on the surface of the soil ball must be teased out, the planting hole must be wide enough for a good supply of planting mixture (see The Pocket Tree & Shrub Expert) and this mixture must be properly firmed down around the plant. Soak the roots of bare-rooted plants before planting if they are dry and make sure to spread out these roots in the planting hole. In the vegetable garden failure to firm the soil around brassica transplants results in blown brussels sprouts and heartless cabbages.

SHADE & SUN DAMAGE

Always check the light requirement before buying a plant. Few plants will thrive in dense shade but a number will flourish in semi-shade. Most plants, however, thrive best in sunny situations — this is especially true for annuals. There are three basic types of shade damage. Stems of affected plants become leggy and the leaves are pale. In addition the number and size of blooms are reduced. The third problem is that the leaves of variegated plants lose their yellow or white colouring. In the greenhouse there is an opposite problem — the need for shading against the rays of the midday summer sun.

WATERLOGGING

The plant is affected in two ways. Root development is crippled by the shortage of air in the soil. The root system becomes shallow and the root hairs die. Leaves often turn pale and growth is stunted. The second serious effect is the stimulation of root-rotting diseases. There is no cure once the roots have been seriously damaged — the answer is to prevent waterlogging. This is not easy if the soil is very heavy and the water table is high — you can raise the bed by bringing in top soil or you can dig in humus before planting. This must be done over a large area — merely putting peat into the planting hole is of little help.

WEEDKILLER DAMAGE

Traces of lawn weedkiller can cause distortion of many flowers, vegetables, roses etc — leaves become fern-like and twisted. Equipment such as sprayers and watering cans which have been used for applying weedkillers should not be employed for any other purpose. Never spray on a windy day.

CHAPTER 10

PEST & DISEASE CONTROL

PREVENT TROUBLE BEFORE IT STARTS

- **PREPARE THE GROUND THOROUGHLY** Pull out the roots of perennial weeds when cultivating soil prior to planting. If the soil is in poor condition you must incorporate organic matter. This will help to open up heavy soil where waterlogging in winter is a major cause of root-rotting diseases. It will also help sandy soil by building up the water- and food-holding capacity.

- **CHOOSE THE RIGHT PLANTS** Make sure the plant is suited to the site. Avoid sun-lovers if shade is a problem, do not pick tender types if the garden is exposed and prone to frosts, and forget about acid loving plants if the ground is chalky. Next, buy good quality stock. Reject soft bulbs, lanky bedding plants and disease-ridden or damaged perennials and shrubs. Look for varieties with resistance to or immunity from major diseases which affect the plant type.

- **PLANT PROPERLY** You have chosen the right plants and the soil is in a fit state to receive them, but trouble lies ahead if you don't follow the rules for good planting set out in the various Expert books. These rules ensure that there will be no air pockets and that the roots will spread into the garden soil in the minimum possible time. Successful seed sowing calls for sowing at the right time into soil in the right condition.

- **REMOVE RUBBISH, WEEDS ETC** Rotting plants can be a source of infection — some actually attract pests to the garden. Boxes, old flower pots and so on are a breeding ground for slugs.

- **GUARD AGAINST ANIMALS** Use netting to protect seedlings, vegetables and soft fruit from birds. A cylinder of wire netting around the trunk is the easiest way to keep rabbits, squirrels, cats and dogs away from the base of trees.

- **ROTATE CROPS IN THE VEGETABLE GARDEN** It is wise to follow a crop rotation programme in the vegetable plot to avoid a build-up of soil pests and diseases which thrive on specific crops.

- **FEED PROPERLY** Shortage of nutrients can lead to many problems — poor growth, undersized blooms, lowered disease resistance and discoloured leaves. Take care — overfeeding can cause scorch.

TACKLE TROUBLE WITHOUT DELAY

- **DON'T TRY TO KILL EVERYTHING** Not all insects are pests — many are positive allies in the war against plant troubles. Obviously these should not be harmed and neither should the majority of the insect population — the ones which are neither friends nor foes. There will be times when plant pests and diseases will attack, but even here small infestations of minor pests can be ignored (e.g cuckoo spit) or picked off by hand (e.g caterpillars, rolled leaves and leaf-miner damaged foliage).

- **SPRAY IF YOU HAVE TO** Spraying is called for when an important pest is in danger of getting out of hand. Pesticides are safe to use in the way described on the label, but you must follow the instructions and precautions carefully. A wide range is offered by most garden shops — look at the label carefully before making your choice. The front will tell you whether it is an insecticide (page 101), a fungicide (page 102) or a herbicide (page 118). Make sure that the product is recommended for the plants you wish to spray. If it is to be used on fruit or vegetables check that the harvest interval is acceptable. Do not make the mixture stronger than recommended.

   The leaves should be dry and the weather should be neither sunny nor windy. Use a fine forceful jet and spray thoroughly until the leaves are covered with liquid which is just beginning to run off. Do not spray open delicate blooms.

   After spraying wash out the equipment, and wash hands and face. Do not keep any spray solution you have made up until next time and always store packs in a safe place. Do not keep unlabelled or illegible packs — throw in the dustbin after wrapping in newspaper. Never store pesticides in a beer bottle or similar container.

- **WATER AT THE FIRST SIGNS OF DROUGHT** The plants should be watered at the first signs of wilting — delay can lead to serious damage or death. The roots should never be allowed to dry out, but daily sprinkling instead of a good soaking can do more harm than good.

- **REMOVE BADLY INFECTED PLANTS** Do not leave sources of infection in the garden — remove and destroy incurable plants when this book tells you to do so.

- **CUT OUT DEAD WOOD** When pruning in autumn or spring cut out all dead and badly diseased wood and burn it. If a large canker is present on a branch of a tree cut back to clean wood.

- **EXAMINE DEAD PLANTS** After lifting don't just throw away plants which have died before their time. Look at the soil ball and the ground which held the plant. If roots have not developed from the original soil ball, make sure you follow the rules for good planting next time. If the roots have rotted consider improving the drainage before replanting. If there is an infestation of grubs in the soil, check if there is an insecticide you can use. Cultivate the area and remove all the grubs you can find.

INSECTICIDES

Insecticides are products which kill insects and/or other small pests. There are three basic types — the product you buy may work in one, two or all three ways.

INSECT-CONTACT TYPES

These work by hitting and killing the pests — they are used against sap-sucking insects such as aphids and capsid bugs. They have no activity against pests which arrive after spraying, so it is necessary to spray when insects are seen and not before they attack. Use a forceful jet and cover all parts. Repeat if necessary as recommended. Examples — horticultural soap, pirimicarb.

LEAF-CONTACT TYPES

These work by coating the insects' source of food — they are used against plant-chewing insects such as caterpillars. They do have activity against pests which arrive after spraying, but the protective cover is washed off by rain. The leaves etc which the insects eat must be thoroughly coated. Spray at the first signs of damage. Examples — derris, bifenthrin.

SYSTEMIC TYPES

These work by going inside the plant and then moving in the sap stream — they are used against sap-sucking insects and some caterpillars. They do have activity against pests which arrive after spraying — in addition they kill aphids hidden from the spray. New growth is protected — complete cover is not essential. Examples — dimethoate, imidacloprid.

THE ACTIVE INGREDIENTS

Many of the products on the garden centre shelves are **chemical insecticides** which are modern complex materials developed in the laboratory and manufactured by large chemical companies. They are safe to use as directed, but the number of active ingredients has been greatly reduced in recent years. Standard sprays of the 1980s and 1990s such as malathion, fenitrothion, bromophos, heptenophos etc have gone. The result is that there are no soil pest insecticides and almost no systemic insecticides. At the same time there has been an increase in the number of **organic insecticides** — fatty acids, derris, horticultural soap, rape seed oil and pyrethrins are available. These are derived from plants — generally less effective than their chemical equivalents but they are acceptable to organic gardeners. For **biological insecticides** you will have to find a specialist supplier — these products are based on living organisms (nematodes, bacteria etc) which are natural enemies of the pest to be controlled. They may be reasonably successful under glass but less so outdoors.

FUNGICIDES

Fungicides are products which are used to control fungal diseases. There are two basic types — the time to put on the first spray depends on the type you choose and the nature of the problem, so it is necessary to read the label carefully.

PREVENTIVE TYPES

These work by coating the plant with a protective coat which kills the fungal spores which arrive after spraying. Ideally the first spray should go on before the disease has started, but in practice the initial treatment usually takes place when the first spots are seen. Repeat as instructed. In a few cases (e.g peach leaf curl) the first spray has to be applied before the disease is seen.

SYSTEMIC TYPES

These work by going inside the plant and then moving in the sap stream. Protection is better than with a preventive type as areas missed by the spray are reached and there may be a minor curative effect on small disease spots, but they will not clear up a bad infection. Repeat as instructed. In a few cases (e.g rose black spot) the first spray has to be applied before the disease is seen.

THE ACTIVE INGREDIENTS

Most of the products on the garden centre shelves are **chemical fungicides** which are modern complex materials developed in the laboratory and manufactured by large chemical companies. They are safe to use as directed. You will also find several **'green' fungicides** offered for sale — these are based on simple age-old remedies such as sulphur, copper salts and tar oil. They are usually less effective than the chemical fungicides but they are generally acceptable to organic gardeners despite the non-organic nature of some of them.

The ready-to-use sprayer is suitable where just a few plants are to be treated

The compression sprayer is necessary where numerous plants are to be treated

CHAPTER 11

GARDEN WEEDS

Weeds are plants growing in the wrong place — they may be wild flowers, grasses, self-sown seedlings of garden plants etc. Last year's tulip growing through this year's wallflowers is a weed. Textbooks stress the various ways in which weeds can harm the growth of your plants — they cast shade, harbour pests and diseases, and compete for water, nutrients and space. The worst effect in many situations, however, is the uncared-for look they give to the garden.

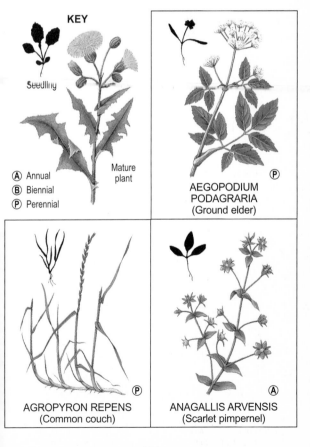

KEY

Seedling

Mature plant

Ⓐ Annual
Ⓑ Biennial
Ⓟ Perennial

Ⓟ
AEGOPODIUM PODAGRARIA
(Ground elder)

Ⓟ
AGROPYRON REPENS
(Common couch)

Ⓐ
ANAGALLIS ARVENSIS
(Scarlet pimpernel)

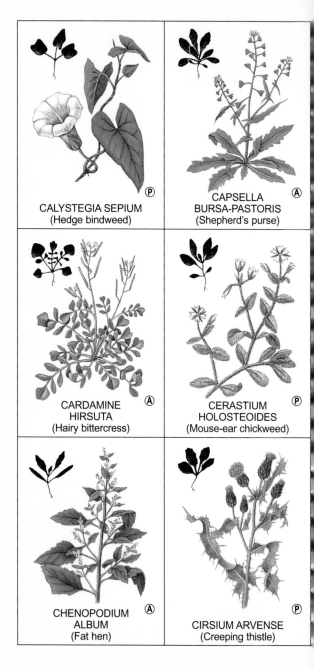

CALYSTEGIA SEPIUM (P)
(Hedge bindweed)

CAPSELLA BURSA-PASTORIS (A)
(Shepherd's purse)

CARDAMINE HIRSUTA (A)
(Hairy bittercress)

CERASTIUM HOLOSTEOIDES (P)
(Mouse-ear chickweed)

CHENOPODIUM ALBUM (A)
(Fat hen)

CIRSIUM ARVENSE (P)
(Creeping thistle)

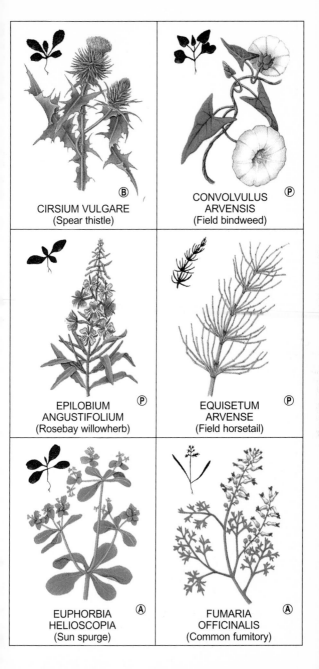

CIRSIUM VULGARE Ⓑ
(Spear thistle)

CONVOLVULUS ⒫
ARVENSIS
(Field bindweed)

EPILOBIUM ⒫
ANGUSTIFOLIUM
(Rosebay willowherb)

EQUISETUM ⒫
ARVENSE
(Field horsetail)

EUPHORBIA Ⓐ
HELIOSCOPIA
(Sun spurge)

FUMARIA Ⓐ
OFFICINALIS
(Common fumitory)

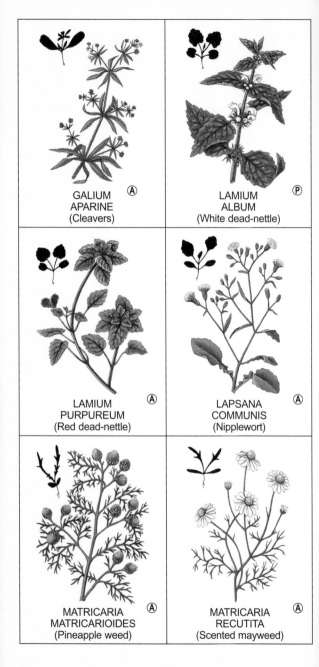

GALIUM
APARINE Ⓐ
(Cleavers)

LAMIUM
ALBUM Ⓟ
(White dead-nettle)

LAMIUM
PURPUREUM Ⓐ
(Red dead-nettle)

LAPSANA
COMMUNIS Ⓐ
(Nipplewort)

MATRICARIA
MATRICARIOIDES Ⓐ
(Pineapple weed)

MATRICARIA
RECUTITA Ⓐ
(Scented mayweed)

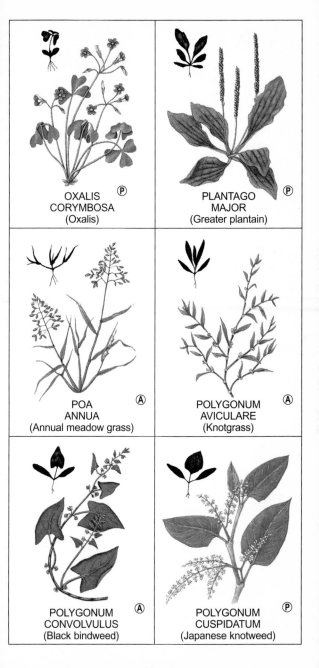

OXALIS CORYMBOSA (P)
(Oxalis)

PLANTAGO MAJOR (P)
(Greater plantain)

POA ANNUA (A)
(Annual meadow grass)

POLYGONUM AVICULARE (A)
(Knotgrass)

POLYGONUM CONVOLVULUS (A)
(Black bindweed)

POLYGONUM CUSPIDATUM (P)
(Japanese knotweed)

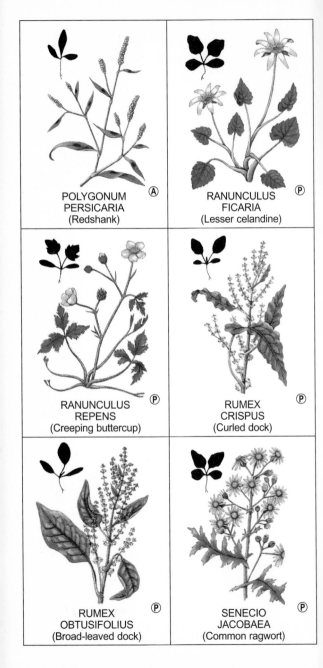

POLYGONUM
PERSICARIA ⒶP
(Redshank)

RANUNCULUS
FICARIA ⒫
(Lesser celandine)

RANUNCULUS
REPENS ⒫
(Creeping buttercup)

RUMEX
CRISPUS ⒫
(Curled dock)

RUMEX
OBTUSIFOLIUS ⒫
(Broad-leaved dock)

SENECIO
JACOBAEA ⒫
(Common ragwort)

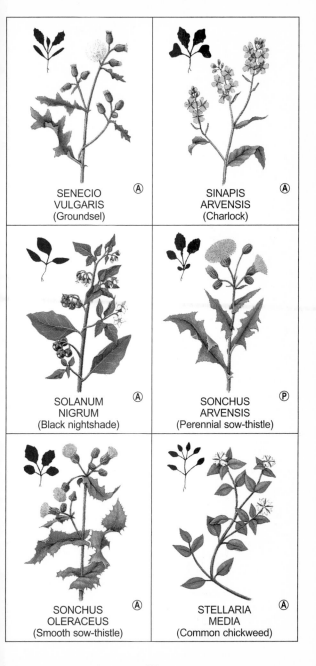

SENECIO
VULGARIS
(Groundsel) Ⓐ

SINAPIS
ARVENSIS
(Charlock) Ⓐ

SOLANUM
NIGRUM
(Black nightshade) Ⓐ

SONCHUS
ARVENSIS
(Perennial sow-thistle) Ⓟ

SONCHUS
OLERACEUS
(Smooth sow-thistle) Ⓐ

STELLARIA
MEDIA
(Common chickweed) Ⓐ

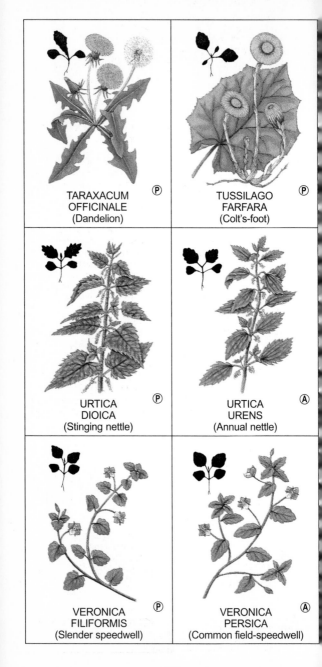

TARAXACUM
OFFICINALE (P)
(Dandelion)

TUSSILAGO
FARFARA (P)
(Colt's-foot)

URTICA
DIOICA (P)
(Stinging nettle)

URTICA
URENS (A)
(Annual nettle)

VERONICA
FILIFORMIS (P)
(Slender speedwell)

VERONICA
PERSICA (A)
(Common field-speedwell)

CHAPTER 12

LAWN WEEDS

It is not unusual to find a wide variety of common garden weeds growing in a newly-sown lawn. When the grass is established, however, the routine of regular mowing brings about a spectacular change in the weed population. Most types cannot withstand being constantly cut down by the whirling blades and so they steadily disappear from the lawn. Many of the hard-to-kill weeds of the bed and border such as ground elder, couch grass and bindweed are unable to exist in turf which is mown regularly.

There remains a small group of weeds with a low-growing habit which are able to survive and spread below the height of the mower blades. These are the lawn weeds — out of the hundreds of weed species which are found in the garden it is not surprising that only a small number are able to exist under such difficult conditions, and the 25 most important and common ones are described in this chapter. In addition there are the grass weeds which call for special treatment and the mosses which are notoriously difficult to eradicate.

There are three basic reasons for a weedy lawn — poor site preparation, poor choice of turf and/or incorrect management of the grass. But in even the best-tended lawn there is nothing you can do to prevent occasional weeds from appearing — wind-borne and bird-borne seeds will see to that. But there is a lot you can do to prevent them spreading to form large patches all over the turf. These will harm the grass and give your garden a run-down look — Chapter 13 shows you how to keep weeds under control.

KEY

CONTROL BY SELECTIVE WEEDKILLER — see page 118

Consistently killed by one application of selective weedkiller

May be killed by one application, but a second treatment is often necessary

Checked by one application, but repeat treatment will be necessary

ACHILLEA MILLEFOLIUM
(Yarrow)

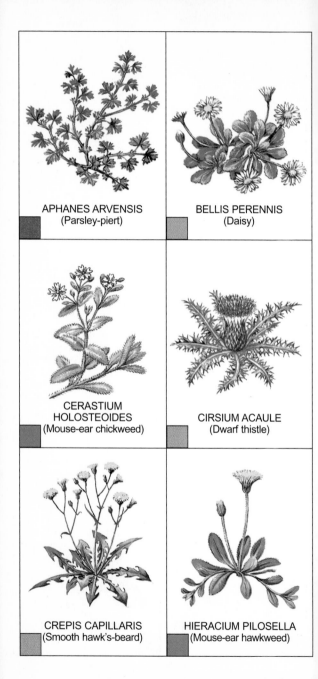

APHANES ARVENSIS
(Parsley-piert)

BELLIS PERENNIS
(Daisy)

CERASTIUM
HOLOSTEOIDES
(Mouse-ear chickweed)

CIRSIUM ACAULE
(Dwarf thistle)

CREPIS CAPILLARIS
(Smooth hawk's-beard)

HIERACIUM PILOSELLA
(Mouse-ear hawkweed)

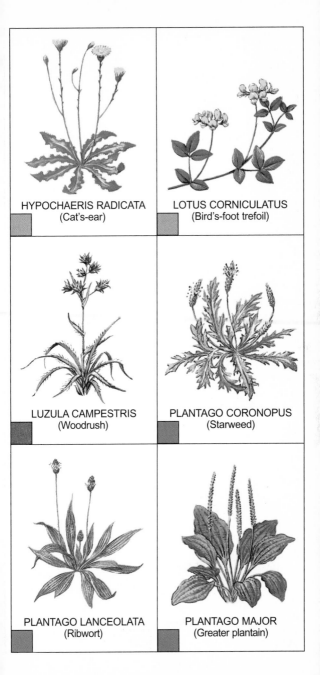

HYPOCHAERIS RADICATA
(Cat's-ear)

LOTUS CORNICULATUS
(Bird's-foot trefoil)

LUZULA CAMPESTRIS
(Woodrush)

PLANTAGO CORONOPUS
(Starweed)

PLANTAGO LANCEOLATA
(Ribwort)

PLANTAGO MAJOR
(Greater plantain)

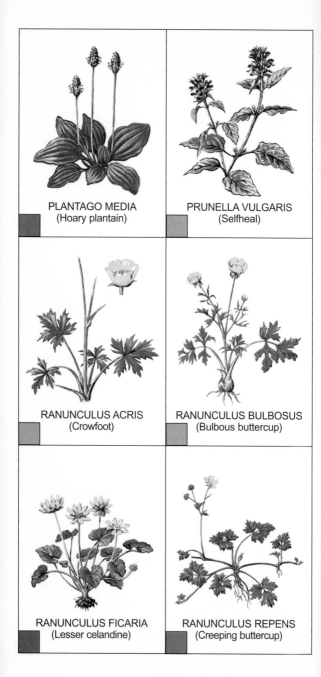

PLANTAGO MEDIA
(Hoary plantain)

PRUNELLA VULGARIS
(Selfheal)

RANUNCULUS ACRIS
(Crowfoot)

RANUNCULUS BULBOSUS
(Bulbous buttercup)

RANUNCULUS FICARIA
(Lesser celandine)

RANUNCULUS REPENS
(Creeping buttercup)

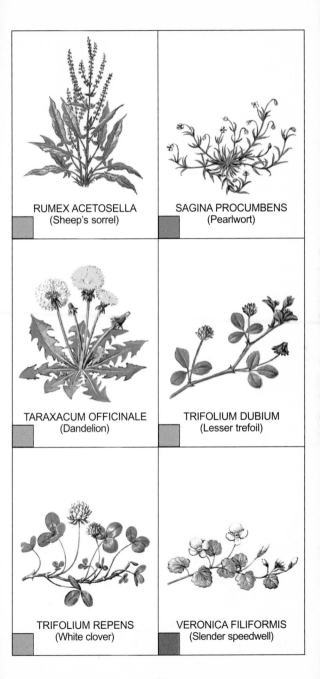

RUMEX ACETOSELLA
(Sheep's sorrel)

SAGINA PROCUMBENS
(Pearlwort)

TARAXACUM OFFICINALE
(Dandelion)

TRIFOLIUM DUBIUM
(Lesser trefoil)

TRIFOLIUM REPENS
(White clover)

VERONICA FILIFORMIS
(Slender speedwell)

MOSS

For many people moss is the worst of all lawn troubles. Remember it is a symptom and not the prime cause of run-down turf. A moss killer is not enough — the only way to ensure long-lasting freedom from moss is to find the cause or causes and remove them. Common culprits are waterlogging, underfeeding, over acidity, shade, cutting too closely, drought and sandy free-draining soil. The type of moss present is a useful indicator of the nature of the problem. **Upright mosses** with tufts of leaves are a symptom of dry and acid soil which drains too freely. On the other hand **trailing mosses** bearing green or golden feathery stems indicate poorly-drained, compacted soil — they can also be a symptom of too much shade. **Cushion mosses** with tiny upright stems are a sign of mowing too closely.

Large patches of moss call for a moss eradication programme which will involve several steps — see page 124. The disappearance of moss as a result of this programme may leave large patches of bare earth before the grass has had a chance to grow back, so reseeding or returfing of the bare spots will be necessary.

UPRIGHT MOSSES

TRAILING MOSSES

CUSHION MOSSES

WEED GRASSES

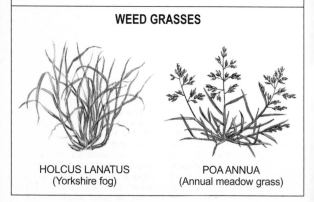

HOLCUS LANATUS
(Yorkshire fog)

POA ANNUA
(Annual meadow grass)

CHAPTER 13

WEED CONTROL

GARDEN WEEDS

Weeding is generally regarded as the most disliked of all gardening jobs. It is a season-long chore and in most gardens it is tackled badly. Little is done to prevent an infestation around the growing plants, and then we wait until the weeds are an eyesore. The garden owner then spends hours hoeing, forking out and hand pulling each bed and border in turn, only to find that the first bed is again full of weeds before the last bed or border is reached.

There is virtually no way of completely protecting your garden from weeds, but you can do much better than the sorry routine outlined above. The answer is to follow a weed control programme which contains several steps — see page 120 for details. The first step is to remember that prevention is better than cure, so take action before the weeds appear. Despite your efforts at the prevention stage some weeds will appear, and it is necessary to deal with them as soon as possible. In all cases the job must be undertaken before annual weeds produce seed and before perennial ones spread. These two types of weeds are treated differently, so right at the start it is wise to discover which types are present (see Chapter 11) and learn the approach to be adopted in each case (see below).

Annual Weeds

Annual weeds complete at least one life cycle from seed to seed during the season. They spread by seeding, and all fertile soils contain a large reserve of annual weed seeds. The golden rule is that emerged annual weeds must be killed before they produce seed — kill them by hand pulling, hoeing or burning off with a contact weedkiller (see page 118).

Perennial Weeds

Perennial weeds survive over winter by means of underground stems or roots which act as storage organs. Dig out the whole plant including the roots if you can. If you can't then the leaves must be regularly removed to starve out the underground storage organs or else a translocated weedkiller (see page 118) must be used which will kill these underground parts.

WEEDKILLERS: WHAT'S IN THE BOTTLE?

A large collection of weedkillers (other name: herbicides) lines the shelves of garden centres in spring and summer. Many contain the same active ingredients but there are still a number of basically different types. You must choose carefully to avoid the twin dangers of killing garden plants and not harming the weeds. There is no single product which is safe on all plants and lethal to all weeds — you will have to choose with care using the guidelines below.

SELECTIVE OR NON-SELECTIVE ACTION?

A **Selective Weedkiller** damages only a limited range of plants — use when the plants in question are resistant and most or all of the important weeds are susceptible. Example — lawn weedkillers (2,4-D, dicamba etc).

A **Non-selective Weedkiller** damages garden plants as well as weeds — use on uncultivated land or choose a brand which can be applied by directed treatment (see page 119) around plants. Example — paraquat.

CONTACT OR SYSTEMIC ACTION?

A **Contact Weedkiller** kills only those parts of the plant which are touched, so complete leaf cover is required. These products are fast-acting and are excellent for dealing with annual weeds, serving as a chemical hoe. But movement within the plant is either very limited or absent, so there is no long-lasting action against perennial weeds. Example — paraquat/diquat.

A **Residual Weedkiller** enters the plant through the roots. These products remain active in the soil for weeks or even years, depending on the chemical concentration, soil type etc. They tend to be unspectacular in action, killing the weeds below ground as they germinate. This chemical type is found in path weedkillers. Examples — simazine, dichlobenil, sodium chlorate, propachlor.

A **Translocated (Systemic) Weedkiller** moves in the sap stream, so roots as well as leaves are affected after spraying. Complete leaf cover is not required. These products are effective against many weeds, but action is often slow and the results are often governed by timing, weather etc. Examples — glyphosate, sodium chlorate, lawn weedkillers.

SPOT OR OVERALL TREATMENT?

SPOT
TREATMENT

Application to a single weed or a group of weeds. Examples are painting the leaves of a perennial weed growing next to a rose with a translocated weedkiller such as glyphosate, and putting a pinch of lawn sand in the heart of a deep-rooted lawn weed. It is useful for dealing with isolated weeds not killed by a previous treatment.

DIRECTED
TREATMENT

Application to a group of weeds, great care being taken to avoid contact with nearby garden plants. Choose a still day and use a watering can fitted with a dribble bar. Examples are paraquat/ diquat in the vegetable garden and glyphosate around herbaceous perennials and shrubs.

OVERALL
TREATMENT

Application to the whole area which has a weed problem. The weedkiller may be a non-selective one where the area is either a path or land not being used for growing plants, or a selective weedkiller where the land contains plants which are resistant to the chemical — for example lawn weedkillers. Be careful to avoid drift outside the treated area.

WEED CONTROL PROGRAMME

① TRY TO PREVENT WEEDS FROM APPEARING The basic reason why you have a weed problem is bare ground. You can hoe or hand pull the weeds around growing plants and in some cases they can be safely sprayed, but if the soil is uncovered then the problem will return as weed seeds on or near the surface and pieces of perennial weeds start to grow. Digging is often an ineffectual way of controlling weeds on a long term basis. The annual types on the surface are buried, but a host of seeds are brought to the surface. With care some perennial weed roots and bulbs can be removed, but all too often the roots of dandelions, thistles etc and the bulbs of ground elder are spread around. The real answer is to try to cover the surface around plants in beds and borders. You can use a non-living cover (a mulch or weed-proof blanket) or a living one (ground-cover plants). Use one of the following techniques:

Apply a non-living cover One of the purposes of a humus mulch is to suppress weed germination and to make it easier to hand pull ones which may appear. This reduces but does not eliminate the problem. Plastic sheeting provides a complete answer — cover with bark.

Plant ground cover Creeping evergreens with leafy stems provide an excellent way of suppressing weed growth around clumps of perennials. With bedding plants you can solve the ground cover problem by planting them closer together than the usually recommended distance.

② GET RID OF WEEDS PROMPTLY WHEN THEY APPEAR Weeds will appear around your plants in beds or borders unless you have put some form of weed-proof blanket such as plastic sheeting around them. These weeds should be kept in check while they are still small. Use one or more of the methods listed below:

Pull by hand The simplest method for the removal of well-established but easily-uprooted annual weeds in beds and borders and the removal of all types of weeds in the rockery. Use a small fork to uproot perennial weeds — don't pull up by the stems.

Use a hoe The hoe is the traditional enemy of the emerged weed and still remains the most popular control method around grow-ing plants. It will kill large numbers of annual weeds if the surface is dry, the blade is sharp and the cut is kept shallow. Hoeing at regular intervals is needed to starve out the roots of perennial weeds.

Use a weedkiller Numerous contact and translocated weedkillers are available for use around growing plants. Make sure you use the right type — see pages 118-119.

LAWN WEEDS

If the lawn has only a few weeds you may be tempted to ignore the problem — from a distance the turf may look uniformly green. It is wise, however, to tackle the problem before it gets out of hand — the visual effect gets worse when the weeds start to flower and the intruders can steadily take hold.

The correct method to use depends on the number and type of weed present. With isolated weeds grubbing out or spot treating with a weedkiller may be all that is needed, but if the trouble is widespread then an overall application of a suitable chemical will be necessary.

After the lawn has been freed from its unwelcome visitors it is necessary to follow the rules of proper lawn care to increase the vigour of the grass and so reduce the risk of re-invasion.

NON-CHEMICAL CONTROL

Non-chemical methods of control are much more effective at the prevention rather than at the eradication stage. Proper mowing is a key factor — cutting too closely or mowing at the correct height at infrequent intervals will weaken the grass and let in weeds. Raking the grass will help to control creeping weeds (see below) but do not overdo it — over-drastic raking can thin out the turf and allow weeds to take hold. Grass will generally recover after a period of summer drought, but if you fail to water then both weeds and moss will find a perfect breeding ground in the thin and open turf once the rains return.

HAND WEEDING

Scattered seedlings of annual weeds can be pulled by hand from the newly-seeded lawn. In the established lawn this technique of hand pulling will not do — the weed has to be dug out. Choose a day when the turf is actively growing. Use a hand fork or a knife and make sure you dig out the root. Keep the diameter of the hole as narrow as possible and fill it with compost when the weed has been removed. Firm down the surrounding turf.

SLASHING

Clumps of coarse grass do not respond to lawn weedkillers. The recommended control method is to slash through the weed with a knife or edging iron before mowing.

RAKING UP

Before mowing rake upright the runners of creeping weeds, the stems of coarse grasses and the leaves of other weeds. In this way these stems and leaves will be cut off by the mower. Use the grass box on a weedy lawn and do not use the clippings for mulching around plants.

CHEMICAL CONTROL

There are two types of active ingredient. The **ferrous sulphate weedkillers** scorch the leaves of weeds and moss but do not go inside the plant — the **selective weedkillers** travel inside the plant and kill both the leaves and roots of susceptible weeds.

A few general rules: Read the instructions and precautions before use • Put on the recommended amount — double dosing can scorch • The soil should be moist and the weeds actively growing • Do not apply in windy weather nor when rain is forecast • Do not mow just before treatment • Store in a safe place when not in use.

WEED TYPE	CHEMICAL	ACTION
LAWN WEEDS These are the non-grassy weeds — see pages 111-115	**FERROUS SULPHATE**	Destruction or reduction of the top growth of many weeds plus moss control — see below
		— or —
	SELECTIVE WEEDKILLER	Destruction or reduction of both top growth and roots of many weeds. More effective than ferrous sulphate, but there is no effect on moss — see page 123
MOSS — see page 116	**FERROUS SULPHATE**	Destruction or reduction of the top growth. Moss will return if basic cause or causes are not removed — see page 124
		— or —
	DICHLOROPHEN	Specific moss killer which is more effective than ferrous sulphate, but it is only available in ready-to-use form for spot application — see page 124
WEED GRASSES — see page 116	—	No satisfactory chemical control is available. Reseed or returf small patches — for large patches slash through the weeds (see page 121) before mowing

Ferrous sulphate

Unlike the selective weedkillers the products based on ferrous sulphate can scorch fine grasses when carelessly applied and they only kill the top growth and not the roots. Despite these limitations a wide variety of weeds, including moss, can be kept in check. Ferrous sulphate is invariably sold as a mixture with fertilizer — when mixed with ammonium sulphate and sand the product is known as Lawn Sand. With ferrous sulphate products apply when the surface is moist and do not mow or walk on the lawn until rain has fallen or it has been watered. Water thoroughly if rain has not fallen for 2 days after treatment. Apply between April and September — the best time is between mid April and early July.

Selective weedkillers

These chemicals, sometimes wrongly called 'hormone' weed-killers, have become basic tools for the care of the lawn. They are selective in their action, killing susceptible weeds but sparing resistant plants such as grasses when used at the recommended rate. In addition they have a systemic action, which means they work inside the weed to kill the roots as well as the leaves.

PRODUCT TYPES

Powder or **granular plus fertilizer**
The most popular way of weeding and feeding the lawn at the same time — a selective weedkiller works better when a nitrogen-rich fertilizer is used with it. A fertilizer distributor is the best method of application — hand application is acceptable but care and some skill are required to obtain even application.

Liquid The quickest way of killing weeds in the lawn. The golden rule is to always add a soluble fertilizer when treating the whole lawn and to never add a fertilizer when treating patches of weed. Mixed products are available. A knapsack sprayer is effective but the tiny droplets are liable to drift. Use instead a watering can fitted with a fine rose or weeder bar.

Spot Scattered rosette-type weeds can be spot-treated with a pinch of a powder weedkiller, but there are special products available for spot treatment. Ready-to-use weed guns and aerosols are squirted into the heart of each weed — wax bars are stroked over the leaves.

NEW LAWNS

Wait 12 months after sowing seed or 6 months after laying turf before applying a selective weedkiller.

ACTIVE INGREDIENTS

MCPA
2,4-D
DICAMBA
MECOPROP
MECOPROP-P
DICHLORPROP

Two or more of these active ingredients will be present in your product.

SAFETY

They will not harm adults, children, pets or wildlife when used as directed, but many garden plants are very sensitive.
Pick the right day (see below), use weedkiller-only equipment and store packs well away from plants and fertilizers.

DISPOSAL OF CLIPPINGS

Lawn clippings obtained shortly after treatment can be composted but the material should not be used for at least 6 months. Do not use clippings for mulching around plants until the lawn has been mown at least 4 times following application.

APPLYING SELECTIVE WEEDKILLERS

Choose a warm and still day with the prospect of fine weather between April and September — mid April to end June is best. The soil must be moist at the time of treatment and the grass should have been mown 1-3 days before. There will be no rapid scorching effect after treatment — control may take 2-6 weeks during which time twisting and curling of the leaves takes place. Some weeds are killed by a single application but with others a repeat treatment may be necessary about 6 weeks later — see pages 111-115.

CONTROL OF SPECIFIC WEEDS

DAISY
An easy weed to control. The top growth is burnt off by ferrous sulphate products, but a more effective method is to use a selective weedkiller. One application may be enough, but if it persists repeat the treatment after about 6 weeks.

CLOVER
White clover is the one you are most likely to find. Rake before mowing so that the stems are brought up to meet the blades. Water during summer drought. Ferrous sulphate applied in spring will burn off top growth — use a selective weedkiller in June and repeat the treatment 6 weeks later. A nitrogen-rich fertilizer will help to keep clover in check.

BUTTERCUP
Creeping buttercup is the one you are most likely to find — a serious nuisance on heavy soil. Isolated weeds can be removed with a trowel or hand fork — if it has spread to produce a large patch you will have to apply a weedkiller. A ferrous sulphate product will check the growth, but it is much better to use a selective weedkiller in late spring.

PLANTAIN
Look for clusters of leathery ribbed leaves with erect spikes of tiny flowers. Greater plantain is the one you are most likely to find, but others can also be troublesome. Dig out isolated specimens — ferrous sulphate has little effect but large clumps are easily killed with a single application of a selective weedkiller.

PEARLWORT
An easy weed to control. The top growth is burnt off by ferrous sulphate products, but a more effective method is to use a selective weedkiller — one application will be enough. It will return unless you feed the grass in spring and avoid mowing too closely.

MOSS
Small patches are not a problem, but large mossy areas are unsightly. Unfortunately there is no easy answer — it is necessary to follow a season-long moss control programme. In spring apply ferrous sulphate — you can use dichlorophen if the mossy area is not large. Rake out the dead moss a couple of weeks later and reseed any bare patches. Feed the lawn in early summer and make sure that you mow regularly at the recommended height — closely shaving the lawn is one of the common causes of moss infestation. Remove shade if at all possible and in autumn rake and aerate the lawn by spiking.

SPEEDWELL
Slender speedwell can spread to form large patches on damp soil, and is difficult to eradicate. Hand weeding is only practical when a few plants are present, and chemical control is generally disappointing. Ferrous sulphate applied in spring will check its growth but there is no long-lasting control — selective weedkillers are even more disappointing. The best you can do is to use a dicamba/mecoprop product and repeat 6 weeks later.

YARROW
A weed of dry and starved lawns — it is difficult to control and no single treatment will kill it. Feed the grass in spring and apply a selective weedkiller when the grass is growing actively. Repeat this treatment about 6 weeks later and again in autumn.

DANDELION
Hand weeding is possible, but a bit of root left in the soil will produce a new plant. Chemical spot treatment is better — for large areas apply a selective weedkiller and repeat 6 weeks later. Ferrous sulphate has little effect.

CHAPTER 14

PROBLEM INDEX

Acknowledgements

The author wishes to acknowledge the painstaking work of Gill Jackson and Angelina Gibbs. Grateful acknowledgement is also made for the help received from Joan Hessayon, Colin Bailey, Ella Norris, Brian O'Shea and Barry Highland (Spot On Digital Imaging Ltd). The author is also grateful for the photographs or artworks received from © Garden Matters, © Garden Matters/ Apps, © Garden Matters/Hoare, © Garden Matters/Milkins, © Garden Matters/Parks, © Garden Matters/Wager, Harry Smith Horticultural Photographic Collection, Pat Brindley and Christine Wilson.

The Experts —
the world's best-selling gardening book